DUANE ARTHUR OSE

ALASKAN Wilderness

ADVENTURE II

OSE MOUNTAIN ALASKA

STRATTON
—PRESS—
Publishing Life

Alaskan Wilderness Adventure II
Copyright © 2019 **Duane Arthur Ose**

All rights reserved. No part of this book may be used or reproduced by any means, graphic, electronic, or mechanical, including photocopying, recording, taping or by information storage and retrieval system without the written permission of the author except in the case of brief quotations embodied in critical articles and reviews.

Stratton Press Publishing
831 N Tatnall Street Suite M #188,
Wilmington, DE 19801
www.stratton-press.com
1-888-323-7009

Because of the dynamic nature of the Internet, any web addresses or links contained in this book may have changed since publication and may no longer be valid. The views expressed in the work are solely those of the author and do not necessarily reflect the views of the publisher, and the publisher hereby disclaims any responsibility for them.

ISBN (Paperback): 978-1-64345-668-3
ISBN (Ebook): 978-1-64345-837-3

Printed in the United States of America

This book is dedicated to Robert H. Sterling, who helped me publish my first book and inspired me in becoming **a writer.**
Thank you, Robert.

CONTENTS

JEFF PETERSON'S TRIBUTE TO ME, THE AUTHOR

Duane, I am proud of you like you would not believe. The setbacks you had, the obstacles you overcame, and the dream you made a reality. I envy you and wish I could live like you do—unencumbered by all the hustle and bustle of city life, where your concerns are more about survival and enjoying life.

If I could make the money I was here, out there, or even close, I would be there in a heartbeat. It takes balls to give up everything to follow a dream, perseverance to succeed, and hard work to make it all come together. This particular book can be your legacy for generations to come, and your mountain only adds to that legacy you have succeeded.

Duane, I look up to you a lot. I am proud of you and wish I could be more like you. My regret is ever leaving that mountain, just to get trapped in the struggles of everyday life. I don't know if I ever told you, but I love you, Duane, and think of you often. You were a father figure when I needed it most, a coach to lead me in the right direction, a team player when we both needed it, and levelheaded enough to think of everything we absolutely could not do without.

This was an undertaking which, under any other circumstances, was doomed to fail. (How many other homesteaders in the area failed?) We made a great team, and I miss that. Whether we were fishing, going on treks here and there, or going to start this wonderful adventure, you were there for me when no one else was, you gave me hope when no one else did, taught me things no one else could, and you gave me an adventure I never dreamed I would get to have! Thanks again!

PREFACE

During the summer of 1986, I prepared to drive the Alaskan Canadian Highway to Fairbanks. This journey would lead me on to a flight to a lake, which had no official name. I had come to call it Levi Lake.

Located near Levi Lake was a newly constructed cabin, built in the year of 1984. The cabin, termed the Frenchman's Cabin, was abandoned at the time of my visit. The cabin was titled this because a twenty-one-year-old Frenchman had built it simply for the sheer experience, as well as building it for an American citizen.

The American failed to meet the Bureau of Land Management's requirements, which I will explain later in this book. That led to the abandonment of the cabin. Only an American citizen could file for a federal homestead.

This young Frenchman built and lived in this cabin. He accomplished that with only a few simple hand tools, within six months' time. When he was finished building, he returned to France, with the experience of a lifetime.

It was this cabin that I would use as a base of operations, during the cutting of an ATV trail to my new land. My new land was located on a hill with the elevation of 1,405 feet.

My land was located 3½ miles away from the cabin. The spot I had chosen was on a naturally inclined ridge, which any road builder would use. The nearby lake would be used as a landing zone for the goods that needed to be flown in from Fairbanks.

Eight Reasons Why I Did Not Choose the Bottomland

I'm often asked why I chose a land far from a lake and high on a hill. The following are my eight reasons why:

1. The high ground had good rich soil, a result of the hardwood forest growing there.
2. The abundant timber.
3. No permafrost.
4. The warm air tends to rise, making the higher elevation warmer year-round.
5. The advantage of drainage from being elevated.
6. No wetland habitat in which mosquitoes thrive.
7. I needed a dryland airstrip in order to land a plane all twelve months of the year.
8. The top of the hill would protect me from the north winds. I selected a specific site that faced the sun, yet was sheltered from the prevailing winds.

The land I found was like a giant, fertile garden bowl, cupped warmly in God's loving hands. The sloping land meant I had running water with the help of gravity, so there was no need for motors or power pumps. I planned to build a pond above and a self-flowing well, which would be made in time. (I am a dowser.)

If I wished to hunt or fish, I could drive to other locations on my ATV or snow machine. Moose not only like the lakes but the high ground as well. Moose are walking meat markets.

Then there is the view of two mountain ranges and the tundra ponds below, to my south. Finally, a dryland airstrip would be usable for twelve months of the year. Using the water landing space restricted my travel to ten months of the year. The land airstrip was needed because I was planning on living here in the future full-time.

I hope this clarifies why I chose the high ground, now back to the preface.

Back home in Wood Lake, Minnesota, everyone knew what I was planning to do. That included a young lad who was nineteen years of age, named Jeff Peterson. I had become a sort of mentor to him, following a harrowing fishing experience. During that fishing trip, he proved himself to be able to face the challenges of an Alaskan trip.

I decided that he would be the one I would ask to spend the next few months in Alaska with me. Jeff had nothing to hold him, nor any responsibilities. When I asked him to accompany me, he responded with "Me? Really? Yes!"

Jeff looked up to me as a father figure. He was also a friend to my youngest son, Daniel, and had heard Daniel recount about his own adventures in Alaska the previous year.

"Jeff!" I said. "I must inform you of what you are about to take on. First, we will fly into the wilderness, land on the lake, and the plane will leave us alone on shore with our supplies. The plane flies off, and when the engine noise of the plane can no longer be heard, you will most likely have the overwhelming feeling of solitude."

"You will hear a suffocating sound of silence, like none you have experienced. This feeling can give you an anxiety attack. It is a scary, never-felt-before feeling. When you experience that feeling, get busy with the task at hand. Otherwise, you could go crazy quickly.

"There is no shortage of work, which is your cure for prevention of these attacks. While it will be good for you to briefly experience the suffocating feeling of total solitude, end this right away. It will only hinder your ability to meet our goals. This adventure you are about to take on will be something you can tell your children and friends about, or describe in a future interview.

"I have come to learn of your cooking abilities, of which I have minimal skills, other than opening a can, or toasting marshmallows over a flame. Your main job, aside from everything else, will to be the camp cook. So help me now in making a list of what a cook will need.

"Last year, Daniel and I traveled light with backpacker's freeze-dried food. That was a good choice for a trip where we were on the move, but this time will be different. We will return each night to a base camp, the Frenchman's Cabin, until we have reached our destination. I will plot the trail at that time, and you can learn how to do it alongside me.

"There are two objectives in making a path. First is to clear trees, making a four-foot-wide path on a marked flagged course. This will take us several days to complete. As every opportunity to easy travel presents itself, we will adjust the route accordingly. It can be straightened out at a later date.

"Second, I will be building a habitable dwelling, once we are on site of my land. It will need to be sustainable for living in year-round. Not simply a wall tent, but a building that will be approved by the federal inspectors (BLM), upon next year's inspection. Building that type of structure will take weeks, perhaps even months.

"I have taken notice of your past work ethics. You, young man, have a fine work record. That is what is needed to get ahead in life.

"I have decided we will be a team. Make sure and pack warm clothes. There's one more thing. We will have a long drive, followed by flying out of Fairbanks to reach our destination in mid-August. The reason I picked that date is during the fall, there are fewer mosquitoes to contend with. Plus, there will be cooler weather to work hard in."

1

Never Drop Anchor in Fast Water

Jeff and I were planning a fishing trip on the Minnesota River, at a place I call the Rock. The Rock was located on the riverbank that was a part of Mr. and Mrs. Leo Wersher's land.

My grandson Darrin Ose "fishing off the rock"

With Leo's permission, we drove on into their pasture. We stopped just short of the pasture fence, along the river's edge. From here we could see the huge broken boulder that jutted into the river.

West of the rock, a hundred yards up river from this boulder, there is a sandbar bank. This sandbank extends about a hundred yards before curving to the west for some distance.

As the bank curves, it turns back to the south, out of view from the boulder. Where the Rock is located, the river flowed generally from west to east, rounding this upper bend to form an underwater sandbar. The sandbar had a drop-off, making a deep fishing hole in front of this massive granite fractured boulder.

I had always wanted to use a boat or canoe to anchor above this hole and fish right over the edge of the sandbar's drop-off. That's where monster fish were feeding. Fishing off the rock was great. From the sandbar's drop-off, fishing would be even better.

Casting off upriver from the sandbar is not an option due to the fast-running, high water current. The sandbar is where the big fish would be feeding on the smaller fish, which were protected from the current.

Upriver, there were two feeder creeks that were home to the bait fish. These bait fish ranged in size from smaller minnows, to larger-sized creek chubs.

We carried the canoe with the fishing gear laying in it. We followed the river's dry, sandy shoreline up to the bend. We prepared to paddle the canoe out to the sandbar, which concealed itself beneath the river's surface.

For a bait container, we had a floating live-minnow bucket full of creek chubs. We had had just purchased these from Delbert and Shirley Welrsann (Del) of Montevideo, Minnesota.

The creek chubs were no less than six inches in length, some were up to eight inches. Del was known for supplying the best bait. To catch big fish, you need to use big bait and have the patience to wait. Smaller bait would be pestered by small fish. The odds of catching a large fish would then be nil, and luck would be the biggest factor in catching a large fish.

There are many kinds of rigging for heavy fish, but we used deep sea rods with as strong of line as needed. We also had black hooks and black steel leaders varying in lengths. This equipment was used to catch catfish, walleyes, and northern pike. The color black, instead of a bright gold color, has proven for me to be the best.

Black is less detectable by the fish that are the size I fish for. The less garbage you have attached on the line, the better. What I mean by that is the larger the fish is, the smarter and more experienced the fish is. Therefore, the fish detects a trap more often than not, thus, using less hardware is better.

I have learned from my experience in fishing a few tips I would like to share with you. First, you unlock the drag, which is adjusted to just short of the rated strength of the line's test limit. With your fingers, hold the line gently to feel the line while fishing. To feed out the line, lightly hold the line with your thumb and first finger. Make sure the drag isn't locked.

Large fish can detect a trap if the bait is tied fast; they can feel that it is attached. Feed out the line ever so slowly; only give out as much line as the fish is pulling. At one point, there will be a pause in the pull on the line. This is caused by the fish turning the head of the chub to swallow it headfirst. Not all bait is bitten headfirst.

After a moment or two, the fish will travel on fast. At this point, stand up, let the slackened line tighten some, and hold the point of the fishing rod toward the water's direction of travel. Be careful not to signal to the running fish. Let the fish think it has a free, unattached chub.

Next, you should quickly lock the drag and set the hook by swinging the rod hard and fast to the side. Make sure you keep the line taut. Never give the fish slack, or it will most likely come loose. The hook may not yet be sunk into the fish.

This is the time where you play the fish out. Never give him a moment of slack because the hook yet could lose its hold. Gain line as the drag setting allows, cranking him to your landing net.

In the case of a monster catfish, while wearing leather gloves, clasp your hand around the fish's lower jaw. Never do this if it is a northern pike.

In the practice of fishing line setups, a good rule is, keep it simple, stupid. In some cases, a leader is not needed, such as with small catfish. Only the lightest sinker is needed, with a black hook tied to the line as is necessary.

The monster catfish have wide, sandpaper-like teeth. When they're thrashing about, a pulling, gnawing action occurs. A plain fishing line will be quickly frayed from its teeth. When the line breaks, you may have lost a monster catfish. Then you would only have a story about the big one that got away.

On the black leaders, I remove hook snaps; only the swivel is left on. This leaves a loop where the snap once was for the hook to be attached to. The eye of the black hook can be bent open slightly by using a small vise grip tool, very carefully.

You then place the hook's eye back on the loop, and the eye of the hook is closed again. Several leaders can be made ahead of time using this method. This saves you time, and you can keep them stored in your tackle box for a quick change of leaders, depending on the different type/size of fish you're fishing for.

For the catfish, I set four inches above the river bottom. I use split shot sinkers for the stops, and various size in weights of sliding egg sinkers. This allows the line to move through the sinkers when feeding out the line. In the fishing for the walleyes, set the sinkers at eleven inches above the bottom.

When I'm fishing for northern pike, I dangle the chub three feet down from the water's surface. I like to use the biggest bobber that is sold. This is because pike come up under the bait.

River sturgeon (up to two hundred pounds) feed off the very bottom with their vacuum extendable mouth, much the same as a sucking vacuum cleaner hose. They use their sensitive feelers, feeding on slugs, snails, worms, and bloodsuckers, which cling on the rocks and old rotting wood.

The old timers called these fish stone rollers. They were dubbed this nickname because they could be heard pecking and moving the rocks in search of food.

Sturgeons move rocks using their spear-pointed, bony snouts. During the night is when you can hear them feeding the most. Night hours seem to be their primary feeding time.

Hanging a lantern over the water seems to attract them. Watch for their antenna, a one-inch, wirelike tip of their tail, which will protrude above the surface like a submarine's periscope. If you see what looks like a tree leaf stem protruding above the surface, moving from side to side, chances are it is an inland river sturgeon just below the surface, attracted to the light.

It has been said that fishing all night is the best time for fishing catfish. It has been my experience, after all my years of fishing for catfish, that idea is wrong. I have found that the best time to fish for catfish is early at dawn, and during dusk into the early night.

This seems to be the case for walleyes too, or at least that has been my findings. At night, you might as well sleep until early light, except in the case of a night lit by a full moon.

Jeff and I were going after the hundred-pound flathead catfish, the largest of the catfish family. It's exciting to have a monster tugging and pulling for an hour. Having the fish run the line out again and again, to bend the stiff rod nearly to a snapping point. Than playing the monster catfish out of the deep, and land him.

When you are reeling in that monster catfish, there is a safety measure you should be aware of before handling the catfish. This information will relax the fish and save you from harm. Grasp the lower jaw of the catfish with your four fingers in its mouth, over the raspy teeth. With your thumb under the jaw on the outside of the fish, poke your thumb upward.

Holding the jaw open paralyzes the fish. Leather gloves would be advised, due to the raspy teeth. Leaving the fish hanging down, remove him from the water and to the shore, or onto your boat. In my case, it was a twelve-foot-long, fiberglass, wide bottom Dolphin canoe.

(The fiberglass Dolphin twelve-foot canoe was given to me in lieu of payment for concrete. This was during an arrangement where I had delivered concrete to a contractor, from my company, Ose Mobile Concrete Inc.)

"Do we have everything in the canoe?"

"I think so," Jeff replied.

"Keep your life jacket close, within reach. We won't actually wear them because the jackets we have are a bit cumbersome for fishing. You take the front, I will shove off. Don't bait up yet. We have to locate the drop-off first, by drifting and waiting for the sound or feeling of the anchor hitting bottom. We will mark it by sight, aligning up with shore landmarks."

The drop-off was where I expected it to be. "Okay, Jeff. We are going upstream, and then drifting back down. I will drop anchor just before the drop-off to secure the canoe."

I lowered the anchor at the spot I wanted, but we did not stop! We floated on past where I wanted to be. The river's current was too fast!

"Jeff! We have to try again. This time I will drop anchor earlier." We made a second attempt, and with my hand on the rope, I could feel the anchor bouncing from rock to rock on the bottom. "Jeff! Here, the river's bottom is rocky, the anchor should catch soon. Be ready, Jeff!"

Suddenly, the canoe stopped moving forward. We nearly fell off our bench seats! Jeff turned back, looking at me just in time to see the river engulfing my end of the canoe, with my life jacket swiftly floating off. In a split second, water was under my armpits, as the bow went high above the water with Jeff on it.

It was like seeing the *Titanic*'s end rise high up before it slid on into the deep. Jeff's life jacket was now gone as well. The canoe was "supposed" to be unsinkable because of the floats built into each end. I guess all bets were off in the fast water.

What had happened was the anchor had caught fast, wedged between the rocks below its rope. At the same time, it was being pulled tight from the strong current. The canoe was seeking the level of the anchor, and it was pulled completely below the river's surface within seconds. Jeff leaped forward off the canoe's bow, which was about to go under. He was closer to the shore than I was.

This was the first time I ever had to swim with all my clothes and boots on. I never felt the cold water, never thought of it. I just continued treading water, making my way toward shore.

I was stuck in the fast moving water but drifting down river rapidly in the current that held me. I was floating along, swimming pretty well considering I was fully clothed, boots and all.

I think the air that was trapped in my clothes helped, but before long there would be no air to keep me afloat. I found myself swimming harder just to keep my head above water, inching my way to shore as I was quickly moving along.

I glanced to my left, away from the river's bank. To my horror, I saw a fourteen-foot-wide whirlpool! It was churning alongside of me, with a small head-sized open hole in its center.

The whirlpool was shaped like a saucer dish, lower in the center by about ten inches. There were ripples like that of draining water in a sink, and it was spinning toward me! The next second, I was in it, sliding to the center where the hole was. I was unable to stop it from swallowing me.

At this time, I inhaled the biggest gulp of air in my forty-four years of life and went down. I was trying with all my might to get back up to the surface. This whirlpool was forcing me down into its drain. I could hear the sucking, rushing, sink draining sound.

My body was down below, inside the whirlpool. I could see my hands extend above the water's surface. While being pulled, I was cupping my hands, grabbing all the water I could to pull myself back up to the surface, but to no avail.

The whirlpool was holding me down. I can swim, but never had I faced this force of water on me, coupled with being fully clothed.

(Did you know the Minnesota River water is yellow and has debris in it?)

Looking up, I could see clear sky above. I was looking at the line of the yellow water's surface, with the clear "air" above. Minutes had gone by. I knew a person's limit is no more than five.

A relaxing, calm feeling came over me. I felt no pain, rather I was very comfortable. I thought of my past in what might have been a flash of suspended time. Then my brain, my real brain, kicked into high gear—the problem solver brain. I thought, *No!* Tomorrow, the sun will shine.

At this point, knowing I could not swim up, I rolled down headfirst. I dove down, touched the bottom, and went swimming horizontally along the river bottom, going as far as I could while holding my breath.

I swam until my lungs felt like they would burst. I turned up, kicking the river bottom with the force of a horse's kick, and mightily pulled on the water to shoot upward. My body shot up high above the surface. I exhaled and took in new air. Gasping, I yelled, "*Help! Help me!*"

I knew Jeff was looking for me. This was my first time above the surface, so I knew he would not know where I was. I was ever so limp, completely exhausted. I found myself floating down river, aside its steep bank. I looked ahead and saw a snag. It was a sweeper with the water boiling and rolling under it.

Knowing I could get sucked under this, becoming trapped, I realized I had to grab on and hold myself there. This, I was able to manage, my legs floated up high under the snag.

I clung on, just resting next to the high bank. I was now near dry land and in time would climb up the bank, after I was rested and had regained my strength.

About that time, I heard Jeff. "Give me your hand." Jeff had made his way down the steeply rooted bank to me. I had known he was okay and had made it to shore early on.

In reply, I said, "No, I am okay. Just let me rest a bit. Then you can help me out of this fine mess."

During the some twenty minutes of rest, relaxing while holding on to that sweeper, a conversation between us ensued.

"Duane! You okay?"

"Yes, just washed and rinsed some, now I know what a wet limp noodle feels like."

Jeff was able to laugh. "Man! Duane, you were under a good five minutes, and I did not know where you were. Then I saw you pop out of the water like a bobber that had been held down deep, exploding above the surface, far down river. I could see you were alive, and then I ran down to help."

"Anything else make it?"

Jeff said, "I got my fishing rod and tackle box, but everything else is gone, the canoe never came back up."

"Well Jeff, one thing is for sure."

"What's that?" Jeff asked.

"Life jackets are to be worn, not looked at."

"You got that right, Duane. And never drop anchor in fast water."

(In my not too distant past, there was a time when I was in a depressed state of mind. This was due to matters of the heart happening in my life. I had thought once, very briefly, of faking a drowning at this same Rock. Then I planned on disappearing in the back mountain country in British Columbia, Canada. I would view my family from afar, knowing that after seven years of not finding my body, I would be declared dead, and my family would get my life insurance. Ironically, at that time, I never did think of Alaska.)

"Okay, Jeff, now I am ready for you to help me up this riverbank."

"It is my pleasure, sir. Our inventories are near zero, but we are alive, and smarter because of this experience."

"Jeff! You have passed the ultimate test. I thank you."

"What do you mean, Duane?"

This is when I asked Jeff, "Would you travel up to Alaska and spend a few months with me?"

Jeff's immediate reply was "Me? Really? Yes!"

"Good! Let us now get on with the next adventure. The drive up the Alaskan Canadian Highway and out into the wilderness of Alaska. Out to my new land."

2

Alaska Bound

The drive up to Fairbanks is 3,500 miles from the Dairy Queen, in Granite Falls, Minnesota. Granite Falls is thirteen miles north of Wood Lake, the town that Jeff and I lived in.

My first experience in Alaska was when I was asked right out of the blue, by my second cousin Mikey Ose, to ride back with him to his home in Wasilla. He asked me to spend the summer of 1982.

Mikey spent the summer showing me around Alaska, then bought my airline ticket in the fall to return to Minneapolis, Minnesota. "Thanks, Mikey. I had a wonderful time and fell in love with Alaska."

In 1984, I once again drove up to Alaska. This trip was after the Wood Lake Public School was out for the summer. This trip, I was accompanied by my son David (then fifteen years old), who had come with me on the drive up.

We traveled in my 1980 King Cab. It had bucket seats and a small topper. David had just earned his driving permit in Granite Falls, Minnesota, after passing the written test.

David's driver license, and how he got it, is a story I must tell you. David, perhaps, is the only person who never had a road test and still got his license. While in Wasilla, Alaska, I took him to the DMV office for him to have his road test.

He was put on a virtual visual driving machine, where he had to punch in the right boxes to answer the questions. He narrowly missed passing his test that day. The next time he went back to be tested, by some act of faith, he was asked on a different machine the same questions.

What are the odds of that happening? David got 100 percent, as he remembered the answers from the last time. They took his photo and stamped out an Alaska Driver's license right there, that hour. When he returned home, he turned in his Alaskan license and was issued a Minnesota driver's license. All this, and never once had a road test.

At the time David and I drove up, there was a woman I had known for a short time previous to this trip. She was a new friend of mine, whom was planning a drive up to Anchorage with her daughter. They would be leaving from the Lower Sioux Reservation, near Morton, Minnesota. After getting to know me, she asked if I would escort them, along with her car, up the highway. We set the date and made the trip.

In the later part of August 1984, Dave, Mike Houseman (who had flown up to join us), and I drove back to Minnesota.

I once again drove up in June of 1985, with my son Daniel, who was fifteen years old at that time. We returned back to Wood Lake in time for his school year to begin in August. This trip, Jeff Peterson and I would be driving up in the early part of August 1986 and staying for an undetermined length of time. We intended on driving back to Wood Lake before winter set in.

Like the last two trips, I had placed three, 2' × 3/4" plywood sections, covering the top and width of the bed of the pickup. The fiberglass topper would sit over the plywood, for us to sleep in.

The topper had sliding windows on the sides, on the back a hinged door, a fixed window at the front end of the topper, and a sliding window in front, which faced the rear window of the cab. Both could be opened to allow me to pass items through the windows.

I could see through to the rearview mirror in the cab. Plus, I had the side mirrors on the doors of the pickup. Having side mirrors was a requirement for me, having only one eye.

24

The three sections of plywood could be removed or shuffled, or all three could be stacked forward to get at the storage in the pickup box itself.

On the topper roof, there was an adjustable screened-in vent cap, which could be adjusted by an overhead hand crank. This topper allowed us to avoid setting up a tent, saving us time. However, the low ceiling height left a lot to be desired. Such as not having room to sit up in bed, we had to crawl in or out.

Having to get up during the night was a pain. So was getting back in, and then having to kill the mosquitoes that found their way in before the topper door could be closed. This was done by burning a short length of a pick coil.

Sometimes, while at a rest stop, we'd open the spring-loaded topper door and lower the tailgate. This gave us a place to sit, eat, change clothes, or search through the pickup load.

I had previously bought in Marshall, Minnesota, a two-wheel tiltable trailer kit. The tires were twelve inches, with one spare tire mounted on a rim. The trailer's box was four feet by eight feet, giving room to haul all the other supplies from Minnesota.

The trailer proved to be well worth the investment; I had no problems in pulling it. While pulling this two-wheel trailer, I learned to keep the front of the trailer's load heavier than the back end. This gave it more tongue weight to keep the trailer from swaying and swinging wildly out of control.

It is advisable to have a road travel guide, such as the *Milepost*, covering the Alaskan Canadian Highway (ALCAN), as well as other travel guides, showing the sites to visit while in Canada. (Nowadays, most everything can be found online as you travel.) During the summer months of the tourist season, every place is open for service, but not in the off-season.

While driving the ALCAN, there could be many places closed. It could be a long ways between gas stations, or any other open places to stop.

During early spring (March) or early winter (October), there could be icy and/or muddy roads, but today (2019) the roads should be in good condition any season. This was not the case in the '80s and '90s. Back then, I drove it many times, sometimes three trips a year. Driving then was fun for me, before they modernized it. I loved the speed-banked cornering, made for the army to travel as fast in the turns as on the straightaways.

Today, with the flattened turns, you best slow down. The first road was constructed hastily, with winding bends, ups, and downs. Those roads were made following the quickest way to build. This so-called highway meant a wild and hair-raising trip. There are places today where this first army road can yet be seen—off to the sides of the current roads.

There are places on the improved road that were once the old one. It's amazing how the road was built and opened in a very short time of six months. In the open flat areas, there were no straight, long, continuous lengths.

The road was purposefully built in a nonsensical way. It had strafing turns (jogs) put in every so often. This was done for the possible air attacks that might have come from the Japanese Air Force. The US Army convoys could use the roads to zigzag their path, to lessen the odds of being strafed (shot). It was all gravel or crushed rock, with some wooden bridges, up until the most recent years.

This army road was extremely dusty, or very muddy. One did not want to be in a tourist camper convoy, up until the newer road was built. Being the lead driver was the place to be, or lagging way behind; others would be eating dirt.

Extra tires, gasoline, and air filters, were wise to have. Following a trip, the windshield was likely to have been cracked several times. It is a badge of honor to have a cracked windshield after you have driven the ALCAN.

Only after entering Canada would I then buy fruit. Crossing the border with fruit is a no-no. Crossing the border was not as restrictive then as it is now. Look into that before you find out the hard way, the dos and don'ts. Get current on the laws of traveling across borders, both into Canada and into Alaska.

If you're not up-to-date on the Canadian rules for visitors, you might be turned back for what you think is a simple thing, and it is not a short drive if you have to turn around. Make sure you have things like photo ID, papers for pets, no fruit, no arrest records, no DUIs, and these rules apply not only for the drivers but for everyone traveling with you. So be well advised, and up-to-date, before you travel.

My old Datsun had over 200,000 miles before it fell apart. It died from rusting out, not from the engine mileage. The body was falling apart. Now I have a 1990 Nissan regular cab pickup. It has a bench seat; it's a plain Jane. It has 89,000 miles on it and runs like a charm.

I've had to replace the battery twice and the tires once or twice, due to age. The pickup is always serviced well. It is not as comfortable riding, as was my bucket seat king cab. When I bought it new in Willmar, Minnesota, I paid $8,000 cash for it. I drove it right off the showroom floor.

I still get thirty-five miles per gallon, and more on the highway, using the cheapest gasoline. It is parked in Fairbanks. I still use it once a year, for a few days while in town. Every time before I drive it, I have thoughts of, let's see now, oh yes, it works this way. It's refamiliarizing, before I run the gauntlet.

For me, living off the grid means really living off the grid. Only while at home on Ose Mountain do I drive much, and then it's on the ATV or snow machine.

(In time, I wore out two ATVs, a Honda 350 CC, an Arctic Cat 400 CC, and a small Elan snowmobile. A snowmobile is referred to as a snow machine in most parts of Alaska. (The native people see the word *mobile* as meaning witch, both in the lower 48 and in Alaska.) We each have a Bearcat Arctic Cat, 4-stroke, wide track snow machines, and a Suzuki 400CC ATV.)

Jeff was shown all the places of interests along the way—museums, viewing point landmarks, flat country, mountain country, oil county, natural gas country, parks, badlands, glaciers, rivers, and lakes.

The people we met along the way were nice to visit with. I would highly recommend a driving trip. Taking your time camping at the many well taken care of campsites, or staying in any of the rooms to rent, or even pull out parking sites. Many are barricaded closed near business campgrounds and motels. There is also the pull-out rest stops used by truckers.

Midway up the Alaskan Canadian Highway, you should be prepared to spend money on expensive food items. For example, I had filled a large, five-pound bag of juicy, plump plums. I went to the checkout, and the young female cashier asked me, "Are you sure you want to buy those plums?"

I looked at the plums. "Why do you ask? They look good to me."

"Oh, they're good, sir. It's just that those are sixty cents each." I then bought only five delicious plums, putting the rest back. A bag of plums would have been something good to snack on during that drive.

One of the places of interest is located at Watson Lake. It's a place called the Mile Post Sign Interpreter Center. Here, signs are brought up by travelers to be hung or nailed up on the walls. This tradition all started as a small thing during the war years, with one auto license plate. Now it is a well-known place.

Stop in and see the signs. There are circles of tall wooden posts on which the signs are attached firmly. You may even recognize those I have put up there, although I am not telling you which signs I put up. You might be able to guess, as I have been around a bit. I have been from New York to South Korea, from Arizona to Nova Scotia, and many places in between.

The place has records in the office to look up. I like the sign with the words "Flushing Michigan" painted on a toilet seat cover. In any case, this is a must stop, covering acres in size—a must see, where you can nail up your own trademark sign. Nowadays, the staff there will place it for you.

At Liard Hot Springs, there is a great campsite and a top-of-the-line place to eat across the road. The campsite has boardwalks that are placed over the marshy, warm waters, trailing to the men and women bath changing houses.

I dare anyone to put their hand in the hottest bubbling spring; a few brave ones do. Liard Hot Springs is a great place. You should plan on spending a full day there at least. Isn't that right, Fred and Jan Cassens of Florida? Fred and Jan were yearly wagon train masters. Rena and I first met them there in the spring of 1991, on our way to Fairbanks, becoming longtime friends.

Whitehorse is a city with a historic gold mining past, on the banks of the Yukon River. Spend time in this robust city. If you need anything, this is the place to buy it; fuel up, rest up, check your rig, for it will be a long stretch before you reach another sizable city with a good-sized airport.

There are no skyscrapers here, but Whitehorse is very spread out in size. There are lots of sites to see and places to eat. It is the last place for Kentucky Fried Chicken. There are just a few towns between the start of the south end of the ALCAN and Fairbanks. That is not to say that there are no other places to get assistance, or tend to your needs.

Small places are well-known for good cooking; the friendly Canadian people will assist you in any way they can. Whitehorse is the place to resupply, as they have more competitive pricing, due to the bulk freighting. You will look long and hard here, for any six-ty-cent plums.

I had made the round trip alone a time or two. I remember once arriving at the border crossing into Canada, in the wee hours of early morning (0200). The female checkpoint inspector leaned out of her inspection window and looked at my large bucket of KFC chicken. That was my trail snack, fresh from Fairbanks.

Drooling, she told me of the last time she had eaten KFC (the nearest KFC was at Whitehorse, hundreds of miles in the distance.) I pulled over, parked, and went inside with the 3/4 full bucket. We shared the remainder. Best stop I ever made. I never did get her name, but thanks, whoever you are.

Border crossings can be located in very remote locations, and the people that work at them rotate their tours of duty time. (See, we did talk some.) During the trip with Jeff, he never had such luck. Jeff was not as fortunate as to have a friendly and up close encounter with a woman. Let alone with a border guard—other than the time we went into a small remote diner and the waitresses wore short miniskirts.

"Jeff, remember that stop?" It was kind of hard to get done eating there. Remote places become well-known. If you see a lot of vehicles out front, there is a good chance that there is a reason they are busy; the food is to die for, and the service is to forever remember.

Haines Junction is another place we would stop to eat, fill up on gasoline, and stretch our legs. Leaving, we had to be sure we stayed on the correct road to Alaska, by turning right. Going straight would have taken us to Haines, and we did not want to travel there. I've heard it's a nice, scenic place, but we were headed to Fairbanks.

Next was the lake named Kluane Lake, with beautiful deep blue water. It has a long shoreline drive, with a lot of tourist shops. Those shops sold diamond willow selections that would amaze you. Campgrounds, motels, and good food could all be found alongside this section of highway. It is hard to cover all the greatness on the ALCAN. I suggest, when traveling this highway, to take your time and not be in a hurry to get from point A to point B—that is what airplanes are for.

Be forewarned about long hours of air travel; it is no fun being crunched and pressed tightly, side to side, sitting straight up, daring not to recline. Being in this fixed position for long hours is like being a sardine in a tin can; the only thing different is sardines are lying down. There comes a time or two when you, or someone in your row, has to get in or out to the isle.

On extremely long flights, the isle is a jogger's walkway to get the blood moving through the veins. The isle becomes full of slow-moving people traffic. Sleep on the plane? Forget that! The only good thing is striking up a conversation with complete strangers, which sometimes are from half a world apart. You try guessing where they are from by their accents, never to see them again once you disembark.

Jeff and I, on the other hand, even when driving for several days, we were relaxed, traveling at our own pace, taking in the sights, and visiting lots of people along the trail. The only cramped space was sleeping in the topper bunk, but at least we were lying down.

I do not care for the bus tours either. Traveling from point to point is fine, but not for tours. Tour buses are extreme in sticking to their schedule, cutting or shaving their time at stops. There have been a few times when I have been at a lunch or dinner stop, and the tables were already set with food and drink. This was before the bus load of tourists had even arrived.

The diner personnel were looking at their watches, marking time, glancing out the windows, walking around antsy like. Suddenly, the bus appears out front. It's then a rush out the bus door, like cattle down a chute.

The tourists enter the restaurant to be seated, eat it now, chew it later. Buy a souvenir on the way out. Back onto the bus, without resting at all, because they were running late.

Hear this: the tour company, whichever it is, gets the bigger cut of the profits. Not only for the customers they brought in, but a fixed percentage of the year's annual take from the businesses they have contracted to stop at.

In my opinion, it is like making a pact with the devil. Ever wonder why some stops see no tour buses? Now you know. Those restaurants and tourist stands have no contract with the tour company. The biggest industry in Alaska is the tourist industry, so the battle of the big boys is on. Everything is contracted.

Some complete tour packages, airlines, boats, and buses, look attractive. You may as well get a book of what there is to see. You will not have the time to take your own photos, unless you just want to show your friends that you have been there.

As you disembark from an airline into an open lobby space, you will see the signs for your tour connection. The rushing tourist herd begins. No cattle prods needed.

Regimental tour bus stops are just that, timely measured. Expect a potty break after standing in line, impatiently crossing your legs, and little time to eat. There is no waiting, and little time to grab a souvenir. You will perhaps find a moment to buy a postcard to stuff in a purse, or send in the mail, when you find the time and the proper postage.

I cannot tell you the number of times I have sat down visiting with dropout bus tourists. It's been mostly couples that have complained about the regimental timing of the tour, and then rented a car to travel at their own pace to see things the tourist bus people would never see, or at least not long enough. If you plan a trip on the ALCAN, you may want to think about this. You may want to change your travel plans, as there is no time for sitting back and relaxing.

A guided mini tour bus, if there are any, would be a better option. That is my advice, having seen the lines backed up in an orderly fashion to use the restrooms in restaurants, gasoline stations, and those fancy built-for-traveler rest stops that are outdoors.

The saddest sight is to see the buses with heads looking out the windows while traveling at 65–70 mph. You will see all the passengers trying to see through or over the trees or from the openings on the hilltops. Curious of what must be out there, cameras outstretched over heads. Jostling to try and find an opening between the fellow tourists.

I have been at some stops when the tourists had learned that I lived out there. It then becomes question and answer photo op time with me. There are even times I get asked for my autograph, or an address exchange. In those instances, I hand them my card.

Sometimes, while I have been seated at a dinner table, chairs move closer, or I have been invited to join them at their table. I enjoy those times and have made many friends along the way.

I especially like the Alaska Railroad and its way of sightseeing. The train takes you into places not seen by the general public. Traveling in an Alaska Railroad dome car, or even in a regular car, you're able to socialize. One can walk about within the entire train.

You can then see and meet the locals that use the train for their needs, called flag stops. A flag stop is where a train is flagged down to stop by local Alaskan citizens going to or from town. They board the train once it's stopped, then mingle with the tourists.

I have never been on a cruise ship. The Inland Passage sounds great to me. You drive onto it with your vehicle, or get on board the Alaska Railroad after you leave the ship.

On the train, you will see some of the backcountry of Alaska. I say some, meaning, you should never plan on seeing it all in a single summer. There is too much to see. Alaska is a big state; plan on a return visit.

I have known some who have been to Alaska seven or more times. Each time they have had a different experience, or saw a different view. Some never left Alaska. They return home only to pack or sell their things. Then return to make Alaska their new home, like me. A very large number of residents in Alaska were at one time military personnel who had been stationed here, or wished they had been.

Jeff Peterson, at the age nineteen, saw his opportunity and seized upon it. I have no doubt that he will go on to have many adventures, but none like the one of 1986—the year he aided and assisted me on my federal homestead.

The Federal Homestead Act of 1862 was signed by President Abraham Lincoln. The act was a breath of life to our nation. It was both an opportunity for individuals to own their own land and for the betterment of a financially healthy, young, growing country. An individual could file for up to 160 acres, paying 12.5 cents per acre. The individual needed to turn the land into a homestead, by measuring the land and making improvements. They needed to build a habitable dwelling and farm on the land while living there. Once those requirements were met, the land was then patented land from the federal government. This meant that the homesteader was the first-time owner of the land. It would not become property with a deed, until the first owner, the homesteader, chooses to sell his/her land. Only then would it become a property with a deed. Patents trump deeds, as the land is owned by the original person to lay claim to it.

Many homesteaders would only claim 20, 40, or 80 acres, but could claim up to 160 acres, as some did. I only claimed 5 acres; it was all I needed. My land is surrounded by federal wilderness, and besides, it is a hundred miles away from a modern road. That made it impractical to own more. I was granted my parchment, called a patent, after I was approved by paying my 12.5 cents per acre and after meeting all the requirements.

Some of the requirements were the following: I had to be an American citizen, I had to be over twenty-one years in age, and because of the bonus of being a veteran, I only had to live on my land for five consecutive months, during one year. I am the first-time owner of this formerly federal land of America.

This land was not previously owned by the state of Alaska. Alaska was purchased from Russia, and the state of Alaska still owns less than 1 percent of the land that makes up the state. My land came from the United States government and the sweat of my brow.

Jeff is now a part of that history, after working with me to establish my home in Alaska. I was the last person to file for a homesteader's claim in the United States of America. My homestead happens to be located on the federal land opening area of 30,000 acres on Lake Minchumina Federal Land Settlement Area, geographically located in the center of the land mass of Alaska.

Tok, Alaska (pronounced somewhat like tow-k, not talk), is the first town after crossing the border on the ALCAN. Tok is a small town where we refueled using American money, once again. That was followed by a good meal while visiting the locals. We then had to make a choice on whether to turn left and head to Anchorage or turn north and drive forward onto Fairbanks.

From this point, traveling down to Anchorage or Fairbanks is about the same distance. I have done both. The drive to Anchorage is a much more scenic drive, but this time Fairbanks was the end of the road for us. Fairbanks is where we would fly to our final destination.

That final destination was a small lake, located below Ose Mountain. Where we were headed is 150 air miles southwest of Fairbanks. I had not named my new land yet. That would come later.

Driving from Tok to Fairbanks, the land geographically is mostly flat. The view offered clear-cut fields for grain farms and hay fields. One farmer had a grain elevator, which was small compared to the ones we passed in the lower parts of Canada. Here, hay fields and grain fields are for cattle and horses.

Fire had killed off the small spruce trees. Fires seem to kill the forests every few years. Only around the wetlands, creeks, and rivers could tall, healthy white spruce and birch trees be found.

In order to make farmland, trees are removed by a Caterpillar bulldozer. The trees are pushed into piles to be later burned, when it is safe to do so. Some of the clear-cuts were fresh, having just been bulldozed. In Alaska, hay is in great demand from the horse ranchers and the dude ranches. Horses are very popular in Alaska.

Further down the road, you can see the buffalo; there are free-range buffalo farms. At these farms, the rancher makes their living from having buffalo hunts and selling the meat. You will have no problem in finding and eating buffalo burgers. You will find them to be delicious.

A permit to kill a buffalo is expensive; I'm not sure about the exact price. The farmers make their living from what the shooter pays, as well as the processing and selling of the meat. For any of you who are interested, check that out. I do quite well in eating moose, but I like the buffalo burger far better than moose meat. Black Angus beef meat, in my opinion, is the best.

Some point after that, we cross the wide but shallow Tanana River. This river flows south, near Fairbanks. It then continues on past the town of Nenana, which is located on its south bank. This river continues on past the outlet, or mouth, of the Nenana River, then onward, empting into the Yukon River. The Yukon River begins in Yukon, Canada, then flows into the Arctic Ocean.

I have failed to mention other towns along the way, but all are great places to see. Twelve miles from Fairbanks, we stopped at the town of North Pole, to go in and see the toys and dolls on display in Santa's House. There you can see the helpers hard at work, answering the big boxes of letters from all over the world. Some of the letters are on the wall to read.

Reading them will warm your heart, bring you laughter, tears, and chills, all at the same time. Letters that are just addressed to Dear Santa, North Pole. The letters come in by the truckloads. The postmaster and postmisses know where to deliver them.

At Santa's House, there are some very fancily made dolls high up on the shelves, along with some very high prices too. They are priced into the thousands, but if you are looking for a special gift, you are in the right place.

We went across the road to a religious radio station, KJNP, 1170 AM on your dial. We were introduced to the people that lived and worked there. This station would be important to us for this is where our families would be mailing their letters. They would not able to call us. The readers at the station would open the letters and read them to us every night after 9:30 p.m., on air.

Jeff and I would not be able to get mail or send mail out. This would be the only way we would get communications for the next few months from home—at least while we would be out in the wilderness. KJNP Radio North Pole is still on-air nightly at 9:30 p.m., but we tuned into KIAM Radio, in Nenana. They have recorded messages from incoming calls, to be played back three times a day—at 10:10 a.m., 2:10 p.m., and 9:10 p.m., save for Sundays.

Heading on into Fairbanks, we pulled up to a KFC fast-food service and ate inside. This place was located on South Cushman, a few blocks south of the east/west Airport Way highway. This highway leads to the Parks Highway, which takes you to Anchorage.

Some roads have been added subsequently. Since that time, KFC has relocated to two new places in Fairbanks. Cushman, in the early days, was the main road and ran right through the heart of town. It still does, but now there are bypass highways on all sides of town. It has expanded greatly.

"Jeff, before we do anything else, we're going to a laundromat."

"Laundry?" Jeff said.

"Then we're going to a car wash, the first thing we do after a trip up the Alaskan Canadian Highway." The rig was coated with mud and dust.

"I can understand a car wash, but why a laundromat?" Jeff asked.

"Here in Alaska, the laundromats have showers too. We need a shower, Jeff. It's about time for a hot shower."

"This is what I call full service!" Jeff said. We washed the pickup, trailer, took our showers, and washed and dried our clothes on this day.

"Now I am going to make a call to Mark Weronko, in Anchorage. To let him know we're here in Fairbanks." I used a common phone booth; back then, they were located almost everywhere.

"Okay, Jeff. Mark will meet us in two days for breakfast at Sourdough Sam's, then again around noon at the Fairbanks International Float Pond. He has a pilot here in town who's going to fly the three of us out. I told Mark how much gear we had to fly out, so he figures we can do it in three trips. Mark has some things he wants to bring out from his cabin, so he wants to share a flight. His cabin is but two miles from where we are headed."

3

Final Days in Fairbanks

The day was late; business places were closed. It was time for supper and make camp for the night, but where? Even late in the day, the sun was still up, so why not see more of the country by driving down to Nenana on the Parks Highway, 50 miles south of Fairbanks? From Fairbanks, it is a 350-mile drive to Anchorage on the Parks Highway, but we were not going that far at that time.

We drove around Nenana seeing the sites and had supper. Much later, near dark, we looked for a place to camp in our pickup. Jeff spotted a dirt road. We pulled onto it and followed it a short distance. We were in search of a place where we would not be seen from the main road, or bother the local people.

This road was becoming narrower and narrower. Any open area was all bushy and mounded with some sunken in depressions. We saw little low fences, like cribbing, and some short wooden crosses tilting. We realized we were in a graveyard, and an old, uncared for one at that.

"Jeff! Get out and help me turn around. We're definitely not camping here."

Jeff was out of the truck, stumbling in sunken graves. We were tripping over those low to the ground picket fences, in the near darkness. There were but a few low mounds. Getting turned around took some time, and so did rocking out of a sunken grave.

When we got out of there, we drove miles back toward Fairbanks and found a truck pull out right along the highway. There might have been the sounds of traffic all night, but no ghosts to bother us. There we crawled into the topper and slept. The next day was going to be a long one; the shopping list was a big one. Most of what we needed we had hauled up from Wood Lake, Minnesota, but we still had a number of supplies we needed to procure.

On the day we went shopping in Fairbanks, I bought 55 gallons of gasoline in 5-gallon gas cans at the bulk plant for $88.00. That came out to $1.60 per gallon.

We also picked up one case of two cycle mix oil, two cases of bar oil, a variety of canned food to include meats, beans, corn, peas, chicken, sardines, cereals, pita bread, peanut butter, jams, jellies, Tang, Kool-Aid, Nestle chocolate mix, sausages, two cases of candy bars, 25 lbs of white flour, 10 lbs of sugar, powdered milk, a bag of apples, a bag of oranges, a 25-lb bag of Krusteaz buttermilk complete pancake mix (just add water), gallons of syrup, packs of butter, 10 lbs of brown sugar, a small lightweight tin disposal, a wood heating stove, twelve feet of black stove pipe, big bags of chocolate chips, cans of mixed nuts, storage containers for the foodstuffs, a brick of 500 rounds of .22 bullets for the Marlin Bolt Action .22 rifle we brought up with us, along with an 8mm bolt-action Mauser Model 98 German army rifle, and five boxes of 20 rounds of ammunition.

I am not sure whether any weapons are allowed, with a permit or not, to pass through Canada. Weapons must be mailed from licensed gun dealer to licensed gun dealer, or carried in the cargo hold of the airline you fly up in.

We had brought summer and winter clothes, two Stihl chainsaws. One was lightweight, with a 16-inch bar for trail cutting. The other, was a heavy-duty size 058, with a 24-inch bar for rip-sawing lumber.

Out on the homestead site, in order to ripsaw lumber, I needed to free hand ripsaw a 2', by whatever width, by 12' plank. To do that, I would need to find a straight tree, fall it, then cut a 12' plus log from it. I would support this log well above the ground at both ends, on short logs I had cut V notches in, for the log to be stable and fixed in place.

I would then trim the high point's top on this log, making it as smooth and straight as possible. Next, with a chalk line, I would snap a line the length of the log, to one outer side. This leaves a blue line for me to follow with my ripping chainsaw.

I would then rest the chainsaw's body against the log, as I cut following the log. This would make a fairly straight cut, and I would remove this slab by letting it fall to the ground.

For the second cut, I would rotate the flat surface to the top on the supporting stand. I then snapped a line near to the right, right to the edge of this flat cut. I sawed that the same way as the first cut, supporting the saw's body in order to keep the cut square.

At this point, I discarded this second cut slab and snap the third line, measuring to keep the cut parallel to the other cut, but as far to the left edge as the flat edge allows. I sawed that off, and now I had a three-sided log. I rotated this timber, measured a parallel line to the now vertical edge, making for a two-inch wide cut. This cut was now my starter plank. Two inches times whatever the first face's flat surface cut was, hopefully being a wide plank of six inches or more.

On the 058 Stihl saw, I had first designed a 3/4" angle iron skid, of 8" in length, and welded it together replacing the tree gripper plate. I attached this angle iron skid using only one bolt with a locking nut. Using one bolt allowed for a changing of the angle, for the best cutting or rocking of the saw.

This angle skid attachment would allow me to ride three sections of four-foot lengths end to end. A 3/4" angle iron, counter sunk and bolted to a 6" × 12" plank, which would be secured by scaffold nails (double-headed nails). The Stihl 058 chainsaw, when sawing, would pull tight the angle irons, like a train on the rail.

In this case, the saw was set up to saw the three sides of a log, thus taking the guess work out, and keeping me from having to follow a line carefully; just nail and cut.

Early on, after I was able to get Mark's Mark III Mill, I found that only the chainsaw mill is needed when resting on a straight, 2" × 8" × 12' plank, in order to start the first cut, or a straight edge of some sort, with a line level attached on the Mark III chainsaw mill. Keeping my eye on the bubble while I was sawing the first cut.

Other items on the list included extra saw chain for both chainsaws, one bar for each chainsaw, splicing links and a tool for splicing chain, two 6" flat millers files, two boxes of round files for the different size chains, three 4' 3/4" angle irons, lopping shears, a double bit three-pound ax, an Estwing hand ax with belt case, a one-hundred-foot measuring tape, a folding grill, a fold up gasoline pressurized camp cooking stove, two mantle Coleman gasoline pressurized lanterns with extra mantles, a case of book matches, one windup alarm clock, one 12-volt car battery, one 12-volt battery charger, one trouble light with extra 60-watt light bulbs, a 25-foot electrical extension cord, pots and pans, a 12" Dutch cast-iron oven, a 5-gallon water jug, canteens, water purification tablets, a water filter, an advanced first aid kit, six red signal flares, bedding, two sleeping bags, earplugs, work gloves, winter mittens, pack boots, a hundred feet of half inch poly rope, 100' × 8' roll of black poly 2 mil sheeting, 100' × 8' of clear 8 mil poly sheeting, three coils of a hundred feet of 3/4" black poly tubing, a case of 25-lb nails, two 2-lb hammers, hand crosscut saw, three sheets of 3' × 3' Plexiglas for making a triple pane window, one 2-foot framing square, a line level, chalk line tool, one try square, a brace and bit with wood drills, 1½-inch wood hand auger (antique), a flat drawknife, a curved log drawknife, a hand plane, a block plane, assorted other wood tools, a toilet seat, a case of toilet paper, a case of paper towels, six feet of insulated 6" stove pipe, two small cans of stove cement, a Swedish bow saw, a map compass, topographic maps, an AM/FM radio, a base station CB radio and antenna, with a $100 handheld forty channel CB radio, $64 worth of batteries for the handheld CB, a $1,600 dollar JC Penney new on the market, shoulder-held VHS camcorder, with eight VHS blank tapes holding a run time of two hours each, three battery packs, and charger.

You might ask how I planned for the supplies needed: I relied on my prior experience in building, camping, survival training, and consulting. I learned a long time ago to seek out information about the things I did not have experience in, like what a good cook needs. This is why I asked Jeff Peterson.

I grew up with a chainsaw in my hands, alongside my dad. I also learned from a good friend, and dealer of Stihl saws, who owns a farm implement dealership company in Redwood Falls, Minnesota.

During my youth, I spent time working with my dad, Clarence A. Ose, who owned a commercial sawmill lumber company. He also owned a farm on two hundred acres. Three woodlots that he owned were passed down from his parents, Knute and Hanna.

Woodlots were for harvesting firewood, as well as lumber logs and fence posts. One of these lots is located on the north bank of the Minnesota River, in Hawk Creek Township, just across from the farm. We could get to it by driving over the frozen river.

A second woodlot was located on the south bank of the Minnesota River, to the east of the mouth of Wood Lake Creek, in the Sioux Agency Township. The third woodlot was found high up above the Minnesota River, on a bluff located in Hawk Creek Township, of Renville County, east of the valley creek. This creek empties upriver from the Rock.

Dad taught me all there was to know about felling trees and making lumber, as well as working for people. My dad was once a Yellow Medicine County commissioner, as well as a local leader. His favorite chainsaw that was on the market back then was the Macula. He swore by it, and it was made in the good old US of A.

It has been a long time since the Macula manufacturing stopped, after being surpassed by Stihl. Stihl is a German product, which works the best for me. Until a day when that brand of chainsaw, too, gets made cheaply. Remember, nothing is forever.

Another way I planned out my list was by going through the house, room by room. Listing what each room might have, or should have. Bathroom, kitchen, bedroom, laundry room, furnace room, cellar, front room, work shop, the list goes on.

Foodstuffs are worked out by the day, the week, the month, and then doubled. Much like the bathroom, where you can never have too much toilet paper, you should have an abundance of food.

There is no running to town when you're in the wilderness. Only a fool brings just a pocketknife and expects to live forever in the wild of Alaska.

This period in my life was not like the other stages when I had a normal pace of climbing the ladder of life's goals. This time, it was a completely new challenge to me—with the addition of being disabled by having a bullet in my brain. This gave me complicated issues to contend with.

The prior experiences I had, along with the foresight to see a second chance, helped me out of the rut I was in. This was a new beginning for me to have an opportunity to do what others only dream of.

(It has been my experience that improving my self-worth financially, and in spirit, should always be my goal, but it is how I manage them both that is important. Living within my means is prudent, much like the comparison of wearing the life jacket, versus sitting on it.)

Base Camp below
Ose Mountain

The evening before we were to meet Mark and fly out to base camp, Jeff and I made camp on the old Nenana Highway. At that time, it was but a side service road in the woods, just south of the Gold Hill gas station and a few miles south of Fairbanks.

That night, while climbing out of the topper to water the plants, I saw that the northern lights were out. "Jeff! You have to see this." Mind you, the night was cold.

We had no heater in the topper, just our warm covers. It was a beautiful view. In the process of viewing the lights, we lost the warmth we had been building up, after we opened the door and uncovered the bunk. We crawled back in and slowly became warm again.

I rolled over, pulling the covers off of Jeff. This made Jeff cold, and of course he had to wake me up to get back his covers. It was a long night trying to keep covered and warm, holding tightly to the covers we each had. Even though the northern lights were a wonder to see, it was cold. That was a long, chilly night, but it would not be our last.

Morning arrived early the next day, and the day would end late. First, we met with Mark in the parking lot and had a big filling breakfast at Sourdough Sam's. When we were done, we pulled into the fenced-in area off of University Avenue, and on to the Fairbanks International Float Pond. Across this long, north/south float pond, and to our west, was where the big airliners were located at Fairbanks International Airport.

On our side of the float pond was the smaller, hard surface plane airstrip. This was filled with small, private airplanes and commercial airline companies. In the state of Alaska, there are more private airplanes per capita than any other place in the world.

The pilot made his preflight checks; one of the things checked on a float plane is to pump any water that may be in the compartments of each float. The floats are made up of several watertight compartments, which have closable openings for a hand suction pump to be inserted. This is usually done by the pilot. On some float planes, the compartments have larger covers for hauling cargo.

Water in the compartments is most often only condensation. This condensation adds up in time, and that needs to be checked before takeoff. It is also necessary in order to keep the parked plane afloat. They are snubbed up on shore for a good reason when not in use. Floats are compartmented for obvious reasons.

The first trip would be taking Jeff, Mark, and whatever else the plane could carry after they were both on board. Each plane type/size has a payload factor rating. The load must be balanced for the best flying during takeoff, the flight, and landing.

This was Jeff's first time on a plane, and he never thought it would be in a plane on water. Jeff told me afterward that he was saying, "What have I gotten myself into?" Sometimes it's best to just jump in, not having the time to worry about how cold it will be.

It is wise to be prepared and concerned, but worrying tends to take your mind off the matters at hand, making your reaction time slow. I learned this during a few close encounters with bears I had—

staying confidently in control, and standing my ground, doing my job. It was only afterward that I started shaking like a leaf in a high windstorm.

Each plane in this international-controlled airspace has to call in to the control tower for clearance to take off. They must call in for landing as well. Being an air traffic control person means working in a highly skilled, responsible position. It's very important for both the pilot and the control tower person to have a clear and distinct voice.

A woman's voice is easier to understand than a man's voice. When I hear a woman's voice in the tower conducting traffic, it leaves me impressed. Those voices should be sold on records for all to hear. Thank you to all women traffic controllers.

The plane, now loaded with Jeff and Mark, was waiting at the takeoff point for clearance. It wasn't long before I heard the plane's engine powering up, and it started making its way toward me. The plane was picking up speed as it was going. I saw one float lift off the water, and then the other. The plane was now gaining altitude, headed for their right turn, and then it turned again.

Soon after the last turn, they were on course for Ose Mountain, leaving the Fairbanks International Airspace. They were still tuned into the aircraft's radio, listening to the control tower. The pilot is always vigil for other airplanes and is always on the lookout for a landing site in case of an emergency along the way.

Emergencies might need a controlled landing. Even after such spots are behind on their course, the pilot still remembers them all. In Alaska, there are few sites suitable for landing. That means most of the emergency landings are really controlled crashes.

All planes are required to have certain survival gear on board at all times. Any landing that a pilot can walk away from is a good landing. Pilots have the final authority to decide if she or he will fly, or are ready to fly. They don't push their limits in order to avoid endangering themselves or their passengers.

Hours passed before the plane returned for me. The first thing we did was unload the pickup and trailer, and then park it in the locked, controlled parking lot. There it would stay until our return in mid-November.

We were in position between the outer markers, waiting. The pilot called the tower to give the lady his call sign, identifying his plane. He gave her the destination and waited for the woman controller's approval. Shortly after, we heard back. "One eight November, float pond one, approved for takeoff."

The pilot powered up, and we headed out past the outer two float markers, on down the float pond, gaining speed. Once the proper speed was reached, one float lifted from the water, followed by the second. We were airborne and gaining altitude. The plane, which had started heading straight, turned right, still climbing. It turned right once more. We were now headed away from the airport, and on toward Ose Mountain.

Flying out to the homestead, I could see the winding rivers and was reminded of that song by Johnny Cash, "North, north, to Alaska. North! To the Russian zone, where the rivers are a winding."

A bit later, we saw the lake we were going to land on. This was the lake where our base camp was located, a quarter of a mile from its west shore. The flight time going one way to the lake is about one to one and a half hours, depending on the wind.

There are five small tundra ponds; there are no official-name lakes on the map, in this thirty-thousand-acre open designated area. The so called lakes have been referred to as Talking Lake, Round Lake, Long Lake, Dead Fish Lake, and Levi Lake. Tundra lakes are made from the glacial ice sheets that have long since melted, millions of years ago.

These tundra ponds are never very deep. The deepest lake, of the five in this area, is Talking Lake, which is one mile in diameter and twenty-five feet deep at its center. The others are only five to seven feet deep.

At the bottoms of these lakes, the ground is frozen solid a thousand feet deep; this is known as permafrost. Wherever there are grassy shorelines, the weeds and grass are heat sinks. The warm sun heats up the plants, and the plants transfer the heat on down to about twelve feet.

The ground is all permafrost out under the lakes. Only a layer of muddy green sludge and duck poop is on top of the permafrost. This soft matter ranges anywhere from four inches to six inches deep, with plant life where the water is no deeper than five feet.

This water plant is what the moose like to wade out to eat. When moose wade out from a grassy shore, they are nearly swimming in the mucky thawed-out shoreline. As they continue out about twelve feet, they are back to being only leg deep because they are on the lake's permafrost hard bottom.

I know this because I, too, have been in the lakes without my clothes. I would wear only a hat to keep my head from getting sunburned. I did this one time for building a dock in the summer, but most times it was for bathing.

The best time to build a dock is in the early days of winter, when the ice is strong enough to support you. You need a platform in order to cut the holes for the posts to be pushed down through. You push them through any soft muck to the hard bottom. These are for supporting the dock above the water.

A dock that will be left out in the lake should be built on the lee side of the lake (west shore) so that the spring winds do not blow the ice to shore. The ice blowing to shore would crush the dock during the spring breakup.

I have often been asked this question: "Are there fish in those lakes?" Yes, but it depends on what you call fish.

These lakes flow into the Wien Lake creek drainage. This creek's headwater is ten miles north of us, and that lake supports fish. Wien Lake is two hundred feet deep at the deepest point. The Wien Lake creek meanders on past us to the south, emptying into the Muddy River.

The Muddy River begins at Lake Minchumina and is the outlet for that lake. Lake Minchumina is twenty-five feet deep at its deepest point. This lake is the largest in acreage size, of all the interior lakes in Alaska. Lake Minchumina is known for its northern pike trophy fishing.

The Muddy River merges with Birch Creek and the McKinley River that is close by the mouth of the Muddy River. They all three flow in the headwaters of the Kantishna River, where the salmon come up to spawn and/or die each year.

The most prevalent fish in these five shallow lakes are what are called mudminnows, or bonefish. The real name is blackfish. These fish survive during the winter by burrowing into the mud bottom and hibernating until the lakes thaw. Some lakes freeze solid, when they are shallow or during the years where the ice is thicker.

When fish die, it's mostly due to the lack of oxygen, which is why they hibernate in order to survive. I have seen a few of the black-fish floating dead. They get no longer than eight inches in length and are all bone. Land otter fish for them, so these lakes make for good otter trapping.

There are northern pike, but only a few. This is due to the water shallowness and lack of decent outlet to allow the fish to migrate when it comes time to head for deeper water. Northern pike are very hard to fish for in these five lakes. That is not to say that all lakes are the same. A northern pike can shut down and hibernate, barely keeping itself alive, once they become ice trapped and have little oxygen available. I have an excellent fishing lake, but it's not one of these five.

One spring day, while on my dock waiting for a plane, I was watching a mallard mother duck with her half grown ducklings swimming behind. Suddenly, without any warning, one of the ducklings was swallowed whole by an alligator-sized northern pike. All that was left was a swirl in the water. The other ducks panicked, moving away as fast as they could.

So yes, there are trophy northern pikes in some of the lake. This one might have beaten the world's record in size. The record-holding northern pike was caught in Finland. I do happen to have a nearby, private lake for easier fishing, which I have made a trail to. This overlooked lake is too small for a plane to land on. It is in this unnamed lake that I plan to catch the new world record–sized pike.

There are other living things in these lakes that will change your mind right quick about dangling your feet in, let alone going for a swim. Two reasons being leeches and bloodsuckers. A time or two now, I have come out of the water covered by black bloodsuckers. Fortunately, they were not on long enough to become attached too well, and I was able to wipe them off.

The leeches are up to three feet in length and one inch wide. I have seen them swimming along, riding the waves just below the water's surface. At first you might think it is a long wide leaf of grass floating along. Do not let this appearance fool you. They will latch on, leaving a mark. After you remove them, you best disinfect the round, red, bloody bite mark, right away. This is one hickey you do not want, nor the memories of how it came to be.

Riding on the plane, Levi Lake came into view. This is where we would be landing, bringing more supplies for base camp. A full year had gone by since I last saw this lake. This time, my trip plan was to begin the proving up process requirements, in order to own the land.

The feeling I had was like reuniting with an old friend. After all, this land spoke to me in mid-July of 1985, saying, "Take me." Not everyone would be a match for this land, but it is just right for me. I saw the future of what it would become. I did not want to change it but nurture a new life of living off the grid.

Once we were on the water, I directed the pilot to the shoreline. We headed to where I had placed a long dead tree, stuck down into the muck upright. I had taped it like a barber's pole in July of the previous year. This was for the point of entry to the base camp.

The cabin was built back in the woods out of sight, about a quarter of a mile away. We saw Mark on the shore's edge, and we taxied to him. At first we did not see Jeff. Jeff bounded to his feet, just as Mark and the pilot started talking.

Jeff had been fast asleep on the soft built up grass. Jeff had not heard the plane fly over, land, or when it power taxied to shore. It was not until he heard Mark and the pilot talking that he woke up. This was a bit concerning to me, as bear approach making no sound. I decided I had better inform Jeff of this fact.

Mark and Jeff had been very busy carrying the supplies to base camp. Hiking back and forth a quarter of a mile, carrying all of our gear, may have been the reason Jeff had slept so soundly. I cannot fault Jeff for that.

The pilot told Mark to stand clear; he was going to drive the plane in tight to the grass so we could more easily unload. That is the point where we discovered that the only one who had hip-wader boots was the pilot. Mark explained that he had four pairs, but they were at home and out here in his cabin. I never had planned on using waders, so I did not have them on the list. There wasn't much that I hadn't thought of.

Mark would be returning to Fairbanks on this second flight with the items he was going to salvage from his failed homestead cabin. He would be helping the pilot with loading up the third flight headed back out to base camp, after they were back to the float pond in Fairbanks.

Unlike me, Mark didn't have a military background. He had to put in four years more time than me, from the point that his habitable dwelling was approved. It ended up not being done on time.

Mark realized he would not be able to complete proving up his time living on site. His job requirements in Anchorage were too time-consuming. He worked as a tractor operator, pulling cargo and planes at the international airport. Mark had the experience of doing his best, all the same.

The cabin and the items left behind would have to be removed. If they weren't, they would be burned by the BLM. The BLM would then charge Mark for this cleanup, to return the site back to nature. That would have been a shame after all the hard work Mark and his wife, Katy, had put into it.

I asked Mark what amount he would take to buy his nearly completed cabin and the items left behind. This would help by saving him from having to pay the government. I could use the logs and anything else left behind.

Without hesitation, Mark said, "Fifty bucks." He told me it would cost him a lot more than that in time and money to make the BLM happy. He went on to tell me that I would be doing him a favor. Plus, I shared the plane trip with him. That way he was able to salvage what he could on that day.

I asked, "Mark, are you sure?"

Mark said, "Yes."

I handed him a fifty-dollar bill and shook his hand, thanking him. Mark's site became my responsibility to restore back to nature for the BLM. In time, this was done, as per the requirements that were set. Wilderness is wilderness.

Mark, his wife, Katy, and their four-year-old son, Toby, had put in a lot of time and effort in this adventure. The cabin alone was a work of love and done well, with good intent. It was not easy for me to take apart their hard work, but I for sure did not want Mark to pay for the burning of it by the BLM.

One winter month, I made a trail overland, crossing the iced-over lake to Mark's cabin. Within a month of effort, I had removed all of his work and restored the land back to what was needed for the satisfaction of the federal government.

In the years to follow, Mark kept in touch with me. Until one day, Katy wrote that Mark had been killed in an auto accident. It happened near the west entrance of Denali Park, where they were preparing a new home to live in. Katy and their son, Toby, were moving to California, where Katy was originally from. That was the last I heard from Katy or Toby. If you someday read this, Katy and Toby, God bless you.

Mark had many stories come from his life—the good times and the struggles here on the lake that I may get into in some later book. One short account I will share.

One time, while Katy and Toby were in town in their home, and Mark was at work in Anchorage, their cabin out here on the lake was broken into by an air pirate. An unknown pilot had landed on water, came in, and stole a generator, two of their family handed-down rifles, and whatever they could carry off of value.

This incident right here, more than any, convinced me that living far from a lake or road was the wise choice. Unfortunately, people, and even some pilots, steal. Bears can be vandals too, but I can kill and eat them.

With human vandals, the flesh is too stringy. So I just drag them off and dump them on top of the ground for the wild animals to share. Within a year's time, not even DNA is left—unlike if a body is buried.

The plane trip that brought me out to the lake also brought the second load of supplies. The four of us quickly offloaded the plane. Mark went with the pilot to his cabin, some two miles away, to salvage his tools and supplies he would be using in Anchorage.

When he was finished, the pilot and Mark would head back to Fairbanks. For the third trip out here, only the pilot would be returning with the final load of supplies, later that same day. The next plane we would see would be the one bringing us back to Fairbanks on November 11, giving us time to accomplish our mission.

After the plane departed the lake and headed to Mark's cabin, we set out to carry the supplies to the Frenchman's cabin. That was the place we would use for the base camp.

To help haul supplies to the camp, and for the transfer later to the homestead, I had made a handcart with one wheel. It was the kind meant to be pulled by one person. This cart was brought up dissembled, and we now assembled it on shore. We were going to use it for the first time hauling items to base camp.

This cart, because of the soft, unpredictable, unstable ground, was a complete failure. We soon abandoned its original function and decided to use it in other ways.

In front of our base camp, I set up the VHS video camcorder on a tripod to record our accounts thus far. I was talking to the folks back in Minnesota about our trip up to Alaska and of our plans. I closed it out when the third load came in, to send it back with the pilot so he could drop it in the mail. It would be viewed later by the folks in Minnesota. I also was planning on using it as a reference for future writing (i.e., this book).

Without the hulk-sized camcorder, I would not have been able to remember much about this adventure in 1986, nor would I have a video with sound recording. I have since converted the VHS tapes to the advent of DVDs for a long-lasting record of history.

Mark had told Jeff and me never to touch any sponges we might find, such as one that would normally be used to wash and scrub dishes. I asked him, "Why not?"

Mark, with a broad grin on his face, said, "You will not find many, if any. If you do find any, keep in mind they weren't used to wash dishes with. Instead, they were used as reusable toilet paper by the Frenchman."

What a neat idea, I thought, *he only had to wash them and let them dry, to be reused.*

"Jeff! How are we fixed with toilet paper?" We both laughed out loud.

August 23, 1986

On this morning, before we left Fairbanks, we awoke to 1/8"
of ice in the low spots around town. Out here it was 60° to 65°
Fahrenheit, just enough for the mosquitoes to be out. They were not
bad, but we were glad we had brought with us a Burgess fogger.

We used it in the camp area later in the evenings. For the best
effect, they should be used in no wind conditions. I had timed this
trip just right—during a season of great weather for working hard,
without having to be sucked dry of blood.

Soon after, toward the end of August, all the wild berries were
ready to eat, save for the ground cranberries. They are bitter before
the frost. Cranberries are best to eat after a hard frost.

After a hard frost, you best hurry to harvest them. The trees
shed their leaves in a matter of days, covering the berries. These cranberries will then be food for the grouse and other animals, all winter
into spring, since the berries will be covered and frozen.

I never liked to eat cranberries until I ate them as an adult in the
wild, right after the first frost. The canned, farm-grown kind that is
made into sauce, to me, is…yuck. Ground wild cranberries (low to
the ground), when served in pancakes, are to die for.

We never fail to pick buckets full of cranberries after they have
gone through the hard frost, and have the best flavor. The time for
cranberry picking happens during late fall (mid-September) on the
side hills, and as early as mid-August in the lower lands. We keep the
cranberries in our freezer during the warmer months and in a storage
container on the kitchen porch during the cold winter.

5

Wild Man Trask

We went to check out what was formerly Mark's cabin, and Jeff had found the valuable triple-paned window of the cabin shot out. We cleaned up and removed the broken glass before replacing it with clear poly sheeting, using some of our supplies. Mark had told us earlier of how it came to be shot out. For the people that lived out this nightmare of a story, it was a frightening experience. No one was killed, but the danger was very real. These guys were crazy, so I'm giving you a warning.

As it happened, after Dan and I had left Mark the summer before (1985), two pretenders were flown into this area and dropped off at this lake. They were pretending to be Vietnam combat veterans and boasted of their conquests. They were nothing more than wannabes. However, these types were not only a great danger to themselves but to Mark, Katy, Toby, and other homesteaders on the nearby lakes.

These two took up residence in the Frenchman's cabin. They had no organizational skills, whatsoever, but were armed with rifles. Apparently, they had known of the open land of thirty thousand acres to be settled in this area but had never looked up the information or bothered with a staking packet.

More than likely, they were thinking of it as free land for the taking. It was as if they could take whatever they liked, drunk on cheap wine, whiskey, and perhaps high from the pretty mushrooms. They would be talking in riddles, firing off their guns indiscriminately, wildly, without any other purpose but to raise hell.

These two became known as wild men. They walked along the shorelines to every homestead claim on these lakes, in search of trouble, food, and drink. One day, these pretenders turned on each other. They started fighting at the Frenchman's cabin, where they were living. The one who called himself Wild Man Trask started firing his rifle after his partner ran out of the cabin.

He began shooting into the cabin when his buddy retreated. After the window was shot out, the firing died down, but only for a short time. Trask returned fire out of the cabin's now empty window.

Understand, this cabin was built like a bunker. Doubled walls, with two sheets of poly in the pole walls, those walls were filled with earth, sort of like a sandbagged army bunker. These walls were capable of stopping, or slowing, down a bullet. However, this cabin was built only for warmth.

No one was shot, but the two split apart then and there. Wild Man Trask held the cabin. The other crazy guy went far away to another homesteader's occupied cabin, to take refuge. I'm not sure on the details from this point, other than what the homesteader has said about not daring to sleep that night.

The homesteader was not about to sleep with this crazy man jabbering, with a rifle in his hands. He was talking to himself all night, on guard with his loaded rifle held in his hands, wielding it about, not being concerned at all of anyone's safety. Sometime later on, the one occupying the homesteader's cabin was flown out, back to Fairbanks.

Wild Man Trask was living at the Frenchman's cabin, surviving on beans and rice that the Frenchman had left there in several five-gallon buckets. (My wife Rena and I found many five-gallon buckets of dried pinto beans and rice that had been untouched, up to as late as 1991.) In time, Wild Man Trask was also flown out by an unknown pilot.

That same day, while on camera, Jeff read the note that this crazy Wild Man Trask left behind in the cabin. The camera starts rolling, recording the video letter that was to be mailed back to Minnesota. Jeff explains to the camera what the note says, with the words and spelling as it was found: "I went to look at the traps, do not enter or will be shoot (yes shoot) on site, signed by Wild Man Trask."

The letter then goes on to say the compass headings that he is leaving from (at the cabin). "I will be leaving on heading 58° NW," and his return headings, "Returning on 28° SE."

I suppose he wrote that in case he did not return. A letter to whomever might come looking for him. He was kind of a dumbass.

6

Third Plane

It was perfect timing. We heard the third plane approaching from the north. Jeff headed quickly toward the lake while I removed the camcorder from the tripod. Leaving it turned on, I ran while holding the camera at my side.

On tape, you can hear me running. All the while I was recording the trees, the tall grass, my rapid breathing, the airplane flying by overhead, slowing down as it prepared to land, and me talking to Jeff.

Jeff was on the grassy open shore so the pilot could see him. Shaky at first, I aimed the camera toward the landing plane.

I became steadier, and I held the camera fixed on the plane landing on the glass smooth water. It was a clear, sunny day. We watched the plane slowly coming to shore. It parked broadside to Jeff, for ease of offloading. I remark on camera what a beautiful sight.

The plane coming in to pick us up in November would be an even better sight. With the November plane's return would be the relief of knowing that our mission had by then been completed. I sign off, saying goodbye to the folks in Minnesota. I removed the tape and handed it to the pilot to mail.

This last load that had been brought to us had filled the plane, making for a long evening of bringing the supplies up to base camp. We dared not risk leaving anything at the lake for the bear to destroy overnight.

7

The Construction of Bernard's Cabin

The Frenchman's cabin was a well-built cabin, which took all of six months to construct before it could be lived in, back in 1984. Bernard, a twenty-one-year-old Frenchman, had done a fine, brilliant job. The cabin was expertly constructed by his assorted wood hand tools.

This cabin was made for warmth and was easily heated with a small disposable wood stove, such as the one I had just purchased and brought along. Because of the way the cabin was built, it was also cool in the summer.

The disposable, lightweight wood stoves were soon taken off the market. They had been deemed unsafe, but to me, that is why it was a disposable stove. It was never supposed to be a permanent stove.

From my past experiences, the style of the building was what I refer to as a Gypsy Cabin. What I mean by that is I had seen in the early '50s, as a young lad in Minnesota, people whom my parents had referred to as gypsies. They were a group of people that traveled the world and the river valley, for fishing campsites.

They would travel place to place in their trailers. Their trailers were rounded, small in size, and easily pulled by a car. Much like the camper trailers of present-day travelers. However, in those days, it was a wagon trailer with four wheels. The gypsy travelers themselves were (maybe?) originally from Romania.

The Frenchman's cabin was constructed with wooden poles made from white spruce trees, varying in diameter from four to eight inches, for easy handling. They were readily growing close by, making for great availability. White spruce is a straight tree.

A single, small diameter pole wall would be useless in the winter. So Bernard, after the floor was laid, made poles that had been draw-knifed, flattened, and fitted. They were placed on top of a poly vapor barrier, on a raised layer of packed earth. This made for a dry floor.

After that, Bernard began building the double walls with four to six inches of space between them, laid horizontal. The inside wall poles were draw-knifed of their bark, smoothed with a carpenter's flat drawknife, and cleaned. The outside wall poles were also laid horizontally, but left with the bark on.

Bernard had brought no nails, but he did bring a wood brace and bit with wood drills. He would use that to make holes where nails would have normally been. He then made wooden pegs for the holes drilled. He also made a sizer for the wood pegs, in order to rapidly make the pegs or dowels.

For all this drawknife work, he had made a drawknife workbench setup. He seated himself on the end that had a foot pedal–controlled clamp. The clamp would hold his work, freeing him to use the drawknife at will.

Clamping the wood meant it was held steady for controlling the wood he was skinning or planning flat. Bernard was a skilled craftsman, with patience. I could clearly see he enjoyed his craft.

In the space between the poled walls, poly sheeting was placed. There was a sheet for each wall, on both sides of this space. This space was then filled with earth, as he built up the walls, all four at the same time. The end walls were set vertical, for the window and door to be placed.

The outer longer walls were built on an inward curve, rounding as they came up. The rounding of the long walls gave them added strength, and thus made the entire structure strong.

Bernard was short in height for sure, less than five and a half feet tall. He was once asked by Mark Weronko, on one of Mark's frequent visits, "Why so short on the walls?"

Bernard said, "Another log is another day, and they are high enough for me."

The roof was a flat roof. It was made up of poles placed ten inches apart, side by side, and peeled clean. On the top, there was placed newspaper printer sheets, which Mark had given him. Thin aluminum printer's sheets, which were used for printing newspapers, are no longer used today.

These printer's sheets were once used as the original print of a full, double page. This sheet was used to transfer print onto the paper. Each page of a newspaper had a printer's plate print, used to print on a page of the paper.

The printer's plates were recycled by sending them to a smelter, to be remade into a blank, clean sheet. One side of the printer's plate was bright, shiny, aluminum metallic. The other side was dull and had the original print used to print each paper on certain numbered pages.

When the newspaper changed this process, it eliminated the need for this printer's sheet. Mark saw a use for the old sheets, to be utilized on his cabin's roof as shingles. Mark had bought the sheets at two cents each and had bought more than he needed, so he gave Bernard enough for his roof's hardened cover. I have a few of these printer's sheets today, and they are forever readable.

Over this aluminum sheeting roof, Bernard had placed a one piece, black poly sheeting, to make it waterproof (flat roof). Over that was placed a heavy, thick layer of moss, a living green moss. At the roof's edges, to retain this moss, were the heavier poles.

The poles on the roof's edges held the moisture that kept the moss alive, giving a great insulation quality that was useful in both summer and winter. Where the chimney pipe came through the roof, there was placed a five-gallon gasoline can, which had a hole cut in the center of each end for the stovepipe to come through. This gave them a metal, empty, noncombustible airspace. It was protruding on the underside of the roof, as well as over the top mossy roof line.

This kept the roof from catching fire from the heat of the stove-pipe. This gasoline can was attached to the roof poles, with metal flashing on the inside around the can, and on the top of the roof for a safe distance. This was wired tightly to the can to prevent water from leaking down the outside of the stovepipe and the five-gallon gasoline can.

Bernard made the door to his cabin out of draw-knifed, square-fitted dry poles, typically braced and snug fitting, with heavy-duty green-colored canvas rolled on the ends for sealing purposes. He made the door airtight with two steel hinges and a metal bolt latch. The door did not need a door latch, unless he was gone. A tree limb handle was used for both inside and outside, to pull or push the door closed; it was that snug.

To go in and out of this cabin, we had to duck down low. While inside, we had to bend over to keep from hitting our heads on the low-poled ceiling, more than a few times forgetting. Jeff and I had no fears from leaving supplies in this cabin while we were off at work.

The Alaskan Window company was located south of Fairbanks on the Parks Highway, near a gasoline station called Gold Hill. That company made triple thermal paned windows, or at least they used to; they have since closed. Before they closed down, I bought some of their windows on sale.

Mark had purchased from this company the window that was placed at the Frenchman's cabin. He had bought it for his cabin but ended up giving it to Bernard. Mark would have given the shirt off his back to help out a person in need.

This window was about three feet by five feet and was installed on the east end of the cabin. Inside was a small narrow table attached below the window. On the outside of the window, Bernard made a heavy-duty, bear-proof log window shutter. You can see through (between) the log spacing. If needed, it could be dropped open on hinges, which were fastened by two wooden pegs when closed.

In 1984, the lake could be seen from this window, but no longer. This is due to the trees that are growing taller each passing year. Today, the cabin is well hidden from view.

I eventually gained a leased trail, going from the cabin to the lake. The BLM gave me the responsibility of its use. Otherwise, they would have had the expense of burning it down and restoring the area back to wilderness.

This five-acre headquarters site was never proved up on. That was the deal Bernard had made with the person who staked it as a headquarters site. It's unfortunate, seeing all the work Bernard had done constructing the building. He made it the best habitable dwelling in the area, at the time.

A headquarters site was on five acres, a homesite was on five acres, and a trade manufacture site (TM) was on eighty acres. One could prove up on all three, having up to ninety acres each. The rules were complicated, and the lands were too far out to be workable, or practical.

In that day and age, not everyone could hold a steady job and live so remotely. Unless like me, a person had a fixed retired income. A headquarters site for a hunting guide had a better chance than a TM site. The latter is nearly impossible to prove up since one needed to show an income earned off of it.

One person tried to get approved for collecting syrup from birch trees. He had the trees on his eighty-acre claim. Unfortunately, the BLM did not accept that plan. Birch syrup is a high dollar seller in Alaska.

The opening of the thirty thousand acres used for the Federal Land Settlement Area, for the most part, was a government farce. The Homestead Act was closed, never to be reopened or tried again. Of sixty-four applicants from this area, I am the only one left standing on my land.

Six of those sixty-four are still owners but are only absentee owners. I do not blame them, for it was but a cruel joke. A costly road access would have been the best opportunity for a sustainable settlement way out here.

There has been the talk of building a road from the Parks Highway, all the way to Nome, and that might happen someday. This would open up the land for people to use, to live on, to work on, for minerals, for oil, for gas—to grow Alaska.

This won't come to be in my lifetime. Only the fortunate few, like *me*, were able to make their homestead work up to the current day, Ose Mountain, a fly-in-only homestead.

Inside this soundproof, airtight cabin, Bernard had a single, narrow, short wall bunk, built for his length. It included an overhead storage rack, too narrow for a bunk. Both were built from draw-knifed poles. There was also a small table made from a draw-knifed flat, and fitted, poles.

Mark pointed out one of the posts that supported an end of the bunk. Bernard called it the snake. It coiled, curving upward, like a raised and flared head of a cobra. Lastly, there was a homemade chair. Its back support was constructed of a bent, small made board. It was a well-made backrest, to fit Bernard's back.

I have never measured the size of the cabin on the inside, but it was 5½' high, and the length was about 12' × 10'. What made it seem small were the rounded walls, low ceiling, and small door. It was made for Bernard, a hobbit's cabin in the wilderness of Alaska. I do hope this chapter does Bernard well, for he must have loved the opportunity to live out a real Alaskan wilderness experience.

Outside near the cabin, Bernard had a hand-dug pond. The pond was made in order to have a nearby water catch basin. It was lined with poly sheeting, which has long since been torn to shreds by bears. This basin was likely made from the earth he used to make the raised earthen foundation and also used this to fill in the space between the inner and outer walls.

The lake was over 1/4 mile of a distance, so he had been collecting water in his pond. Also, Bernard had built a very high cache to keep things safe from bears while he was in the process of building. I saw the claw marks from more than a few bears that had tried to climb it.

Bernard had wrapped steel high up around the trees that were used to keep squirrels and bears from climbing into his cache. I can only imagine he had some vandalizing bears to contend with, and Bernard was without a gun.

8

Lake Viewing

It is not hard to understand why people love to live on the shores of a lake. The seasonal views alone are a strong magnet for living on a lake shore. If it were not for the many reasons I spoke of before, about why I chose the place I did to build my home, I would have chosen a lakefront property on which to stake my claim.

Water is a magnet to wildlife and people. Beaver, moose, ducks, geese, swans, eagles, mink, otter, marten, lynx, wolverine, fox, weasels in the summer, becoming ermine in the winter, muskrats, shore birds, and even the rare caribou. They all migrate over the frozen ponds, using the ice for shortcuts.

During the month of August, we saw the ducks, swans, sunsets, sunrises, and the distant Alaskan mountain range.

Here are a few views:

9

The First Five Days

The Frenchman's cabin was uniquely situated for base camp, with a gradual incline to my homestead. Any other location would have meant traveling on the low wet ground, then up steeply to the homestead. Those routes may have been shorter, but to a road builder of an all-season trail, those locations made no sense.

One night, after Jeff's well prepared supper, we went over the topographic maps to lay out the proposed route. Topographic maps do not show in detail the dips and curves, but we got a general idea of the attack route we would set upon.

The next morning, the first thing we did was set up a rainwater catch basin before the rains would come. With this, we would be prepared by having fresh, drinkable, safe water for our needs for the coming weeks. This collection system was set up on the north side of the cabin. We used the north wall to attach a clear, eight feet wide piece of poly sheeting.

It would go from the cabin's top edge to the ground, extending the poly outward. The extended sheeting was then moved aside, to allow for the placement of logs that would form the holding pond. The poly was then attached to these logs to form a squared holding pond. Now it could rain during the nights, and be clear during the days.

The next five days, we scouted, marked with flagging, and chainsawed to clear a trail one and a half miles up from base camp. By the way, the rain catch basin we had just made on the first night proved itself by being full of about sixty gallons of water. "Thank you, God."

There was no reason to hike all the way to our destination. Instead, we foot by foot cut a trail. This was to be a permanent route, and to zigzag to get there would be a waste of time. This was a lesson I had learned after my time up there the previous year.

This trail I planned to make was going to be from four feet to over five feet in width, when completed. It would need to accommodate a 4×4 ATV. This was preparing for the next year.

That is not to say there were no obstacles to clear as we advanced. Mind you, no standing and usable timber was fallen. We encountered deadfalls, heavy, thick new growth of standing trees and dense brush.

When it came to the sinkholes, we deemed it best to give those a wide berth. They were expanding in diameter. The sinkholes were forming from ice melting beneath the ground, which was covered by mosses, ash, and windblown sand. Some sinkholes had whole trees caving into them.

The recent forest fires of fifteen to fifty years ago had areas of entangled mixes of dead, burned falls, which had rotted on the ground. Some were waist-high, with new trees growing up through them. This made three-dimensional puzzles, chainsawing through that was a blur of work.

I compared this task to a samurai swordsman in a fight of never-ending death. Clearing away all this kept Jeff busy. I had chainsawed everything I could into short lengths, turning about every once in a while for those I had missed.

Jeff kept up with me and gave me no time to rest. We both were hard workers. It may have come from my bossiness in my army days, but we had done well together.

To those that have never seen the aftermath of a forest fire, it might come as a surprise that fire kills living trees, but they are often left still standing. They are left to rot, eventually falling to the ground. It's usually the underbrush and deadfalls that get turned to ash. When there are merging fires, a firestorm is created. Firestorms leave behind only ash and some burned stumps.

Burning cleans the forest of undergrowth and mosses, as well as killing the trees' harmful insects, which multiply in the rotting wood and attacking other living trees.

To prevent an out of control wildfire, it's best to set small fires from time to time. This is called a controlled burn. Controlled burns are done by the experts, who use the evenings or wet days, when there is no wind. Days with high humidity work well too.

The fire control teams always keep water close at hand, to wet the burned embers. They work generally at night, with the drip torch personnel in the lead, along with the people holding the water-pressurized sprayers.

Rotting dry wood on a forest floor is nothing more than a tinderbox waiting to explode. When a wildfire burns through an area previously burned by a controlled burn, the trees remain alive and the homes around them are safer. Proper fire management and control saves lives and dwellings.

Not all forest fires are put out or stopped from advancing. If they are deemed to be of no threat to private property, or human life, they are left to burn. It is Mother Nature's way of life, as it has been since before mankind.

The rain comes soon after a fire, to wash the air clean, making the cycle of life rebound anew. On the same token, mankind is part of this world. We must find ways to adapt and live together, but not like cavemen. We need to improve humanity and leave it better than we found it so there can be harmony.

Sinkholes come from the glaciers that had been covered by dust and volcanic ash millions of years ago. Through time, it has thawed from exposure, after the earthen moss cover had been burned away. Bears are known to use these sinkholes to hibernate during the long nights of winter.

Remember, most of this land is permafrost, which may be over a thousand feet deep. At one time (or many times), the earth had been near what is known as absolute zero. Only on the sun-exposed hillsides would wildfires of millions of years ago manage to melt some of the permafrost, at least near the surface.

By test core drilling deep into Iceland's, one can find non-ice material. This part of Alaska is semi-permafrost land.

On earth's surfaces of barren soil, past or present day, the first thing to grow when conditions are right is the ground mosses. They are the first to appear. The other plants follow, eventually growing to a point where trees can take root.

This happens after there is ground cover, to provide moisture to support the trees' roots. There is ice beneath much of this area that will never thaw. If heavy earth-moving equipment should unearth a glacier, it is called a pingle.

Sometimes, what looks like a hill is nothing more than ice that had first been covered by ash and windblown drifted sand, with no foliage or trees. At least four times in earth's history most of the land was frozen and covered with ice and snow. The region that I live in the center of Alaska was an arid land. At one time in history, Alaska was much like the Sahara desert is today. This was long before the Ice Age, but Alaska has been very volcanic in the distant past.

In the cutting of this trail, Jeff and I had become road builders, using an ax and shovel in places. Where there were sharp dips to fill, or as needed, we cut into the high side of the steep side hills. We did this at places where the trail would parallel the side hill.

We cut into the sides until we could make the trail either head upward, or downward, but not tilting. That would leave a fear of tipping over an ATV, or snow machine. Wherever possible, we stayed away from having to move earth to level the trail. For the most part, we avoided this extra, time-consuming work.

In very few areas, before we would climb to high, dry ground, we had little choice but to cut a wide trail over wet muddy ground. In those places, we filled the cut in with logs that were then pressed, or jiggled, into the mud. They were put six inches deep, preserving them. Otherwise, if they were exposed to the air, they would soon rot.

Wood fence posts rot six inches above the surface and six inches below the surface. Making the trail wide in the muddy parts meant, later on during the wet season, I would not have to use the same route twice. Also, it brought comfort knowing there is a bottom, for the future use of an ATV.

When I saw this muddy terrain, I knew then that an ATV would require having a twenty-five-foot electric cable winch to attach to the existing trees on the trail's edge. Placing heavy logs in this muck meant less time in drying up this muck. This experience I had learned from my dad and brothers, whom had built roads and farmed near mucky bottoms.

Each day, we would bring the camcorder and the .22 rifle. I ran the camera, and Jeff was always alert for fresh meat, which most often was one of the four different breeds of grouse in this area. A fifth breed, the prairie chicken, is found in Canada and other parts of the lower 48 states.

Most commonly found here are the ruffed grouse, and followed by the spruce grouse and willow grouse. Last is the flighty ptarmigan grouse, which turns white during the winter months. Ptarmigan's meat is white and the tastiest. It was no matter; Jeff made them all good to eat. I had taught Jeff how to aim well, and make each shot count, while we were back in Minnesota.

The first three grouse I listed are easy to kill with the toss of a stick or rock, if you can find a rock. This area is covered by volcanic ash and windblown sand; there is no rock on the surface less than eight miles in any direction, and often beyond. The only rock that is exposed has been covered by flowing water or is at the limits of the falling volcanic ash fields.

Those birds are dumber than a box of rocks. Their idea of being safe was to fly up off the ground into a tree. If several were in a single tree, Jeff would simply use the .22 rifle and shoot the ones at the bottom first. He would then work his way up, killing only enough for our needs. He left the others for a later date.

Jeff shot them in this order because he had soon learned that shooting the one on top was like scoring a strike when bowling. The top falling dead grouse would cause the ones below to fly away. Additionally, they had to be shot in the head. If they were shot in the breast, they still sat until they died. Jeff was quick to learn this, about where to shoot them.

While I am on the subject of grouse, I feel the need to inform you of my experience in eating this bird during early spring. Like most animals, there is a season, for a reason, to hunt and eat the wild game. This is more evident in the eating of grouse, or at least that is what I found.

I learned this lesson the hard way. To survive, there are times where you will need to kill during any season of the year. One time, I had killed and ate a grouse during early spring. Soon after eating it, I became very sick, a nauseous, icky feeling.

Since then, I never kill or eat anything during its breeding/rutting season. Even big game tastes best when the breeding season has passed. Eating that spring grouse made me ill for days.

10

The Events of the Next Fifteen Days

August 29

It had been five days since we arrived at the base camp. We had been busy working in the same clothes every day since we had our showers in Fairbanks. With the abundant water supply close at hand, Jeff decided this was a laundry day.

It is not like I am afraid of work. There are just some things, like doing laundry, cooking, cleaning house, and fixing the bed, I avoid like the plague. I only do that work when I have no other choice.

While Jeff stayed back to do the laundry, I took the .22 rifle, a roll of red surveyor's tape, a canteen, a dry trail snack, and the camcorder and headed back up to start laying out and marking the trail. Making myself useful by doing the work I am accustomed to doing.

Jeff stayed back at the cabin, armed with a scrub board, washtub, clothespins, a clothesline tied to trees, and a pile of sweaty, dirty clothes. Life is not always a bowl of cherries.

As I made my way up the cut trail, I thought of the many people that have spoken to me on how they love the great outdoors, camping, fishing, and hunting. For the most part, these activities get a person back in their comfortable beds at home by nightfall. Other times, people stay in a fancy travel home for a weekend. Others might spend a longer time at some well-kept campground, with all the facilities one has at home.

For sure, most people are rarely ever in the wilderness for longer than a month, with a supply of clothes and food. Yes, the Great Outdoors of Today. Grizzly Adams would be shocked to see how living in the great outdoors is done today. Mind you, I am all for improving the lifestyle.

Until you have lived while enduring the old ways, you have not really lived. I thank God for this chance to know firsthand. Not by choice so much, but out of the sheer will to survive. I hope I am a good example.

When I reached the end of where we had stopped cutting earlier, I began working my way inline, keeping the cut trail to be flagged, as straight as I could. The thick stand of healthy birch made it hard for me to see any further than twelve to twenty feet at a time.

I found it easier not to go far ahead before I could tie a flag (using surveyor's tape). Keeping three flags in view at all times, I could then look back. Looking back worked best for keeping the train inline.

I was being careful not to go off to the sides of the forested ridgetop. I was staying on top, or as near as I could. In order to see where to flag, I stayed closer to the west edge of this wide ridge. Following it gave me the best direction of the actual terrain, which was thickly forested.

Suddenly, I came into a moose yard. Not a fenced-in yard but an area that had shorter trees, which made for easy browsing. When I say moose yard, I mean this yard was like a well-used livestock yard. Only a very few of the trees were yet standing.

Earlier, I had placed the camcorder on the ground at the end of the trail already cut, in order to continue on flagging and marking where the new trail would be cut. If I only had the camcorder with me the first time I entered the moose yard, I would have had some footage of two moose just off to my side. They thought they were hiding from me by dropping down and lying on the ground in place, instead of running off.

It was kind of funny to see big full-grown moose lay still, thinking I could not see them. Hiding like that is what they were taught while they were young. I made my way to the camcorder and brought it back, but the moose had since moved on.

I did, however, take footage of the yard and of the trees that the bulls had smashed flat. It was as though the trees were but toys for exercising and rubbing their antlers.

Looking at my watch, I called it a day. I made my way back down toward base camp. While passing through the Enchanted Forest, a big porcupine was waddling down the cut trail ahead of me. "Fresh meat!"

This was the only thing on my mind at this point. Aiming carefully, I killed the porcupine with one shot. No big deal, it was an easy kill. If it were not for the fact that fresh meat meant so much to us, I would not have shot this porcupine. Instead, I would have taken action footage of him using the camcorder.

When I got near camp, Jeff saw I had something. "What's that?"

"Porcupine," I replied. "We are going to eat good tonight! It will be like eating pork." Or so I had heard.

Jeff had all the laundry hanging on the line. I took it upon myself to field dress that fat thirty-pound porcupine. Removing the prickly hide was a trick, but I got it done without getting stuck with quills.

Unlike what you may have been told, porcupines do not throw their quills. When the porcupine's attacker, or threat, is very close, he slaps/snaps his tail. The quills are thrust hard into whatever is threatening the animal. Once the quills are driven in, they are released, detaching from the porcupine.

Come supper time, Jeff had done a very good job cooking that porcupine. It looked well basted, browned, and was tender. At first bite, I recognized there was a different taste about it than I had ever tasted before. That was to be expected.

I was putting it down, not hungry like, but just being nice. It was not that delicious and tasted somewhat like pine pitch. Yeah, like pine pitch. Then again, this was an animal that ate the bark of the spruce trees. Of course it would have the taste of spruce.

I said to myself, *It's cooked meat, I can do this.*

When I was nearly done eating my fill, Jeff went and asked me, "Would you like an *arm*?" Okay. I was done. It was time to move away from the table.

When Jeff asked if I would like an arm, that just grossed me out. It was hard to keep down what I had just eaten. That was too humanlike for me. Never did we kill another porcupine. (A spruce tree is not pine, but spruce is comparable to pine.)

August 30

We wondered how far in miles that we had gone in the cutting of our trail. Jeff tells me, "We do have a hundred-foot measuring tape."

"Oh, that's a great idea! Jeff, would you care to hold one end while I hold the other? That way we can measure our cut trail?"

"Nope," Jeff said.

"Okay. I thought so, but how about using a wire?"

"A wire?" Jeff said.

"Yes, we will measure a wire one-fourth of a mile in length and attach a rounded knob as a stopper at the trailing end for an inserted ground pin. It will have an eyelet to catch once the knob end is stopped by the eye pin and pulled out with a noticeable tug.

We had several eye pins for the ground wire to travel through. Each time one was driven into the ground meant another quarter of a mile had been measured. The knob at the end would be the stop on this wire. Then the next pin would be inserted into the ground; so on and so forth.

The hard part was remembering to record each stop. The wire measuring would give us an accurate measurement in land miles. This we did being careful not to forget to keep count of each quarter mile measured. In my past, I had measured land this way.

This measuring of the trail eventually led to us naming the different landmarks, or the mile markers, like those you see on the sides of a highway. This one would start from the lake, mile zero.

1. The Dock
2. Frenchman's Cabin
3. Muck Hole
4. Little Forest
5. The Enchanted Forest
6. Tank Trap
7. Mile One
8. Rifle Alley
9. Moose Yard
10. West View
11. Hangman's Tree
12. Mile Two
13. Grizzly Bear Crossing
14. Eagles Roost
15. Mile Three
16. Brauzers Bridge, then finally
17. Ose Mountain

With the wire measure now set up, we headed up the trail measuring. I could not help but think of the critters seeing this wire. Watching it slithering on up the trail, wondering what kind of critter that was.

While Jeff had done the laundry the previous day, I had marked out a good distance, which was ready for this day's cutting. When we cut into the moose yard, again there were moose to be seen. Some were hiding, laying down when they saw us approaching.

A cow and her calf stood back up and walked on by us. Using our newly cut trail, the mother moose stopped and looked back, as if to say thank you. I captured these moose on the camcorder.

This area was an easy cut. I cut while Jeff went on marking the trail ahead. Later, Jeff came back telling me he had seen a really big bull moose. It was not too far from him, but the moose walked away.

Nearing the end of the day's work, we plodded back to base camp. We had time for Jeff to prepare supper while I sharpened the saw, preparing for the next day's cut.

August 31

After a hearty pancake breakfast, we headed back up the trail. This time we brought with us a fold up camp grill, a five-gallon gasoline can cut in half, and the fixings for a dinner on the trail. This half of a gasoline can, which had been cut to make a short can, was to be used for making our cooking fires.

We were using the short can in order to contain the fires. It also allowed us to put them out without worrying about setting the mosses on fire overnight. There is no rock in this area to make a safe firepit on, or to contain a cooking fire.

To cut and remove the moss tundra would take some time. Even then, it would not be safe because of the root system from the moss. It would become a smoldering fuse. Without an excess of water, we couldn't drown the ashes to cool.

So this metal container was very important, for there was no abundant water source nearby to use for our daily trail cutting cooking fires. All we had was the water we brought with us.

The measuring of the trail using the wire worked very well. This wire was pulled along each morning. As we got up to continue cutting, we would measure starting from the place we left off on the previous day's cut, continuing on until it was time to retire from the new day of work. I kept a record in my shirt pocket notebook. (People who have known me forever know that I always have a notebook in my pocket.)

Now all we needed on this job was a timekeeper and a flagging woman for traffic control. Well! The moose were using it as we were working on it, and I am sure other critters were too!

Jeff grabbed the .22. "What's up, Jeff?" I asked. He whispered to me to be still. Quickly, I turned on the camcorder, following him into the bush. I tried to follow him pointing the camcorder his way.

Stealthily, Jeff moved further into the thick trees. Jeff was looking upward, he took aim, and I heard a shot. Crack! He emerged holding a ruffed grouse. I held the camcorder and recorded this moment.

This bird would be eaten the following day. You never eat your catch the same day, as you might think. Grouse is best after its cooled one day. It would be field dressed immediately and kept until it was time to cook it. This, too, came from my experience.

We returned to cutting and clearing trail, until it became time for Jeff to make dinner. Dry cooking wood was gathered, a site on the trail was selected, and the fire container was loaded and set afire to heat up. The grill supporting the kettle was placed over the fire.

Jeff got to measuring out what he needed, and we sat and waited. Visiting, trying not to watch the water come to a boil. There seemed to be a problem with keeping the fire hot, and I saw right away what the problem was.

There were two things: the wood was a little damp, and the fire can needs an air draft under the fire for a hotter burn. I pulled out my hunting knife, and Jeff placed his boot against the can on one side. I lined up the point of the knife on the other side.

Once we were ready, with my closed fist, I hammered the blunt butt of the knife. This drove the sharp point into the can's lower side. Now we had an air hole for a draft, but more were needed all around for the best burn. When we were finished, we had a good cooking fire can—like an outdoor grill.

After dinner, Jeff marked more trail. I kept sawing, removing what had been cut. The rest of the time Jeff was right behind me, tossing and stuffing the fallen/cut trees into the tight, thickly wooded edges. To find a place to shove a tree was not all that easy, and an opening soon became packed with the trees that Jeff stuffed in.

Jeff was always looking for a new place to push a tree in, off the cut trail. If a tree was not pushed far enough off the edge, it could in time come back in on the trail.

Jeff ran into the same bull moose a second time that day. This time, the moose held its ground. Unafraid of Jeff, he continued to munch on the treetops. Jeff acted in kind and continued on flagging the trail.

Jeff and the bull were now getting to know each other. This bull moose had a seven-foot wide rack, a very impressive moose. Its track imprints were as wide as two of Jeff's size 11 shoes, placed side to side. I estimate this moose to be all of 2,500 pounds.

At one point, Jeff added up the number of the different individual moose he had seen while marking trail. He counted slowly, thinking as he counted, of thirteen different moose. We called it a day and headed back to base camp.

September 1

The 1/4-mile wire was pulled forward and recorded, and then I readied the chainsaw. Each night, we left behind on the trail our tools for cooking, the mixed chainsaw gasoline, and the bar oil. The gasoline and bar oil is hoisted high into a tree with a rope, where a bear cannot climb or reach them.

Bears love all plastics and any petroleum products. It is the thick oil that bears like the best. Heavy bar oil makes for good, tasty bait, which bears can smell from long distances. If we were to leave one drop of bar oil on the ground trail overnight, a bear would find it. A hole of two feet wide by a foot and a half deep would be awaiting us in the morning.

This happened more than once. Oil is the best bear magnet I have ever known. It works overnight, and the bear will keep coming back for more.

The day was going along very well, and it was hard work. It felt good to look back at the trail we had cut each time the chainsaw ran out of gas. At noon, Jeff fixed three grouse, making for a big meal. After dinner's rest, we resumed cutting the trail.

The chainsaw had to have the chain tension adjusted often because of the constant use stretching out the chain. This Stihl saw had but one flanged nut and stud bolt holding the bar because it was a smaller saw. I liked it because it was nice and light.

I was often loosening the bar's flanged nut, then retightening it. I was in the process of doing this when *snap*! The stud bolt broke clean off, flush at the surface of the chainsaw's body.

I was prepared for replacing chains and bars, but not a stud bolt. Had I thought ahead better, the chainsaw would have had two flange nuts with two stud bolts. Lesson learned.

The broken stud bolt was the only thing wrong with this saw, but that was all she wrote. Now what? We still days of trail work ahead yet to do. I knew what had to be done, but it would not be much fun for my back.

I would have to use the 058 Stihl chainsaw, which weighed twenty-five pounds of dry weight. The 058 saw had a larger-sized chain, and the bar was 24". For these trees, the power was unlimited, allowing me to cut trail even faster.

It was only the idea of being bent over all the time, while holding twenty-five pounds, that I wasn't keen on. In my past, I was a twelve-inch concrete block layer; those weighed twenty-five pounds each. Not hard to work with normally.

Laying that first round of blocks while being bent over, and having my head down, was not fun. I was not looking forward to spending time bent over while working like that again.

My day of sawing was over, but I went on to finish up clearing off the trail while Jeff went on out ahead flagging trail. I told Jeff, "If you see that bull moose again, act normal and let him feel safe."

I could hear Jeff mumble to himself, "Yeah right!" I laughed, knowing he would be okay.

September 2

The first day of using the 058 Stihl, it was a tree falling machine. The only thing missing now was a wood chipper set up for Jeff to toss the trees into, as I virtually mowed them down.

I found it easier to be on my knees. Sort of walking on my knees, ducking as the trees fell. Sometimes, three or four would fall at a time, flooding Jeff with the work of moving fallen trees off to the sides. Stuffing them would be a better statement.

At times I would get up, turn back, and recut the trees that had fallen beside Jeff, narrowly missing him. Jeff was always alert.

In all this cutting, we never once cut into a wood-rotted beehive. Cutting into a beehive would have been disastrous. Mind you, this was always on my mind. It kept me alert.

It was near the end of the day, and I was cutting trail. Jeff was ahead of me marking the trail for me to cut the next day. There was a long distance between us, so I didn't know what Jeff had experienced, until we were back at base camp having supper.

During our midday trail dinner the next day, I set up the camcorder to record our dinner—especially Jeff's moose encounter story.

I wish you could hear him tell it with sound in this book; the camcorder was set up and rolling during the preparation of noon dinner. When the time was right, and we had our bench made of fallen trees, I asked Jeff to tell me about his previous day's close bull moose encounter.

Jeff began by saying, "Well, you know we have been seeing him and his lady friends for the last what, three to four days now? They have become unafraid of us. The noise of the chainsaw and the other noises from us have not bothered them. They like our trail and use it like the edge of a dinner table for self-serve diners. We could go into business collecting moose nuggets, shellacking them, and make moose earrings to sell at the tourist shops. Yesterday, I was flagging trail when the big bull moose showed up again, just a short ways ahead of me."

I asked Jeff, "How far away?"

"Oh, I'd say maybe fifty feet, thereabout," Jeff replied. "We looked at each other a few moments, and then both of us went about doing what we were doing. The bull moose, eating treetops, and I kept flagging the trail."

"Then what?" I asked.

"He turned toward me, not mad or anything, but just wanted to come my way. The trees were thick, and I did like you had told me."

"What was that?" I asked.

"To act normal, let him feel safe. He and I knew each other. He was bigger than I, so he had no fear of me and came on toward me. I had the .22 rifle, but I did not want to hurt him. Nor could I have. The trees were so thick, I could not swing the long rifle very easily."

I said, "Not much choice for you, Jeff, but what happened then?"

"I pushed my back into the trees, and then looked up into his eye," Jeff continued, using his left hand held up high above his head, over to the one side, saying, "One half of the moose's rack was over there."

Jeff's other hand went up high, showing the other half of the moose's rack passed above his head, extending behind him. "His eye was big, and I saw myself in it. Like those round mirrors in the stores. His rack of antlers was all of seven feet wide, and it was above my head at least two feet. (Jeff was all of six feet tall.) The bull never stopped walking. Traveled right on by to a juicy tree, and ate the top of it within a few feet of me. When he was walking by, I felt the ground move, and I heard the crunch of his hoofs snapping the dry sticks."

"What else did you see when he was walking past you?"

While he was looking at me, Jeff's immediate reply was "I saw steaks, roasts, top sirloins, sausages, and hamburger." (That's one DVD recording I will never get tired of watching.)

September 3 through September 11

Things were uneventful for the most part, except for getting further away from base camp. That made for longer trips back and forth to work.

As we worked our way uphill, the land started to have a steeper incline. We were about to enter part of an old growth forest. All the birch leaves were turning a golden yellow. It was a beautiful forest.

Together, we agreed to name this forest the Golden Forest. This place was familiar; I had seen it in 1985. A strong, warm feeling came over me. I knew that any day now, we would be on my land, our final destination.

One of the days during this time, I was at the upper end of the trail and I came upon a porcupine skin. I thought it strange to find only the skin, until I saw the tracks left by its skinner. The tracks were not very detectable because of the ground cover.

I found upon closer inspection, long, three-inch claw impressions, from a padded grizzly track. It did not take long for me to realize, then, we were not alone. Jeff and I were not the only meat eaters in the woods. A grizzly had killed this porcupine and had skinned it cleanly. I found the skin in one piece; it was not shredded.

In this part of the interior, the grizzlies are not brown like those that live on the edges of the ocean feeding on salmon. Here, grizzlies are silver-tips. This name comes from their silver long-haired humps, and gray outer hair, with black underhair.

They're all of four feet wide, and when they run down our trail, their bodies touched each side. When they ran, they looked like a moving shaggy-haired carpet, like rolling waves of water moving on effortlessly. In the years to follow, I saw more than a few. (Two up close and personal grizzly bear encounters, to be covered in a later book.)

September 12

Each night, we tuned into KJNP 1170 AM radio at 9:30, out of North Pole, Alaska, hoping we would get mail sent to that station that would be read to us on air. There were a few letters, but not enough according to us. My mother, Adora, and my son Dan were good about sending us letters. There were also a few others.

On the previous night (the eleven[th], Mom sent us a nice, informative, long letter stating all was well. It is comforting to get mail for moral support when time and distance is a factor.

Years before this, when I was far away serving my country, a letter at mail call that had been in route days for weeks was like a treasure to be held close to the heart. To read and reread sometimes in the letters would be a personal gift with meaning—like a lock of hair, photos, or even a pressed flower.

Those were the days that few will ever know since the advents of new technology in communications. Technology has made communication quick as the speed of light, being the biggest factor. Next will be the electronic particle teleport machinery that will send items and or people to planets light-years away, hopping planet to planet, stretching the human life span into infinity.

This was an important day to us, for Jeff went on ahead to do some scouting up into the Golden Forest. He returned with great news. "Duane, someone has been here before us!"

"What did you find, Jeff?"

"I found a line of saplings that had been broken or bent, about waist-high, coming from the west. The path continues on eastward, according to the way the trees were bent."

"Jeff!" I announced cheerfully. "We were here! That is how Daniel and I marked that section of trail last July 15, 1985."

Upon Jeff's report, I immediately went off to the east side of the trail and found a tall full-grown birch tree. I climbed high up to the uppermost branches to have a look. From that vantage point, I could now make the plan of attack for the final approach.

We would gradually cut trail curving upward, to the right, following the inclined hillside terrain. Then we would go more to the right, completing a 90-degree turn. At this point, the path leveled again, paralleling the south facing hillside. This continued on to the ridgeline of my homestead claim. This will make a well-engineered trail to drive on in the years to follow.

The fall colors of the Golden Forest were impressively welcoming to us, on this day. It was like a sign of good things to come. Our pace quickened all the more, knowing tomorrow would be a new type of work, with a new challenge.

Tonight would be like the night before a beachhead landing, having great anticipation, checking and rechecking our gear, for the longest day ahead.

11

Trail Complete

September 13

We carried full packs for camping in order to take and hold the ground. After establishing a final working camp, we would then complete the trail.

Working our way as planned, cutting this section snug to the baseline of this new hill side, which we called the Golden Forest (fall colors of tall birch trees), we were heading to our left but gradually climbing as we cut.

As we were about to turn sharply to the right, the marked route Dan and I had made came into view. It was perfectly in line, merging with the trail we were cutting.

About a hundred yards later, the 1985 blazed trail dropped down too steep for an ATV trail. Jeff and I continued on the grade best for the permanent trail. Seeing this marked and blazed trail, which Dan and I had made in July 1985, was refreshing.

Jeff and I walked it; I was showing Jeff the blazed trees we had marked in the making of this trek. In 1985, the trees had been blazed by me, chopping the outer birch bark deep into the heartwood (the point where the inner bark covers the heartwood). I did this for longevity, to scar shoulder height on both sides, the one we approached and on the opposite side, as we traveled forward.

The reason I marked the trail in this way was to see the trail coming and going. There could be a time when we needed to make a retreating trip. I also did it in case a search party would come looking for us.

My brother Michael, who was nine years younger, had this thought. He wanted everything to be prepared, in case Daniel and I did not return by a certain date.

About a foot lower down on the birch trees from where I had marked with my hand ax blazing, Dan used his knife to peel a strip of outer bark two inches wide. This made a black ring that can still be seen today.

We used this method to mark the trail in 1985, after we left the shoreline of Lake Minchumina. My "Independence Day," July 4, 1985. You can read all about this in my first book, *Alaskan Wilderness Adventure*, sold by Amazon.com.

In addition to blazing this trail, we marked each campsite. We usually did this by leaving a rectangular, igneous basalt, which is black stone. Fire altars is what we termed them. We came closer to my new earthen firepits, where the rock had been covered by volcanic ash millions of years ago.

The exposed rock was seen only at Lake Minchumina, and the first three quarters of the trail Dan and I had blazed the year before. This trail is fifty-seven walking miles long, and about thirty-four air miles to my homestead claim. This rock is deeply covered ten air miles south of my land claim. Only in the creeks and high cliff walls did we see exposed rock, from that ten-mile point to here.

Alaska has been very volcanic in some areas, having deep wind-blown ash fall, which covered vast regions of land. This has happened not just once, but several periods in time. I discovered this during my extensive digs, although I found the area of Lake Minchumina relatively free of any heavy ash falls.

Even as recently as the summer of 1993, I was dumped on with a 1/8" of volcanic ash. The ash came from a volcano eruption that happened south of Anchorage. That was approximately four hundred air miles south of Ose Mountain.

That day, I first saw the plume rise high into the stratosphere with no sound. It rose up, looking like an atom bomb blast. A moment later, I heard two big booms. *Boom! Boom!* The plume rose higher into the stratosphere, drifting with the high altitude winds.

Two days later, the sky became extremely dark, nearly black, during the day with no sunlight. Gray snowflake-like, whitish, ash cinders were floating down from the darkened sky, like small gray grains, or like the ash from a forest fire. This ash was crystallized sharp needles, as well as flat sharp sickles.

Some particles had landed on my paralyzed eye, the only working eye I had left. I could not feel anything in my paralyzed eye. This was due to my head injury back in 1977, but I could see the ash particles up close.

I went inside and washed, flushing the eye. This ash was stone ash, which was a very abrasive pumice. You could have used it for polishing a shine on metal.

In a matter of hours, this fallout of ash made everything gray. The trees and ground were covered, and not until the rains came days later was it cleaned away.

The rains made the air safe to breathe, as well as making it safe to walk outside. The rain helped keep a damper on the gray, dusty foliage. Nor did I think it wise to run any motors. That ash fall was only an eighth of an inch.

I have since dug down and found one ash fall to be nine feet deep. Dividing this nine-foot gray ash layer was a thin, but distinctly black, ash line of burned vegetation. Beneath that burned blacked vegetation of ash was a second volcanic drifted gray ash of fifteen feet deep. Under that, the land turned into bedrock—right here on my land.

The ash makes for easy digging and has no permafrost areas. It does, however, have a near freezing temperature. The only way for me to find rock is to dig deep or in the places where water or winds have eroded the ash. Hills are made up of either rock, or glaciers, covered by windblown, drifted ash dust and sands.

After Jeff and I had walked this section of our blazed trail from 1985, we went on to finish up cutting the ATV trail. What was left to do now was to go from the ridgeline to my homesteads claim. I went ahead to look this land over. It was the first time for Jeff, and the second time for me.

The ridge that runs through the center of my claim has a clear and well-used game trail. The trail leads up to the top northward, from the bottomlands to the south. This narrow ridge was a natural for having an animal trail. Every creature used this ridge trail and probably had for millions of years. Mammoths to mastodons and migrating caribou would have used it. It was like an animal highway.

I showed Jeff where the log house would be built while standing on the very spot. This crest overlooked a drop away hillside of two hundred feet, then on to a more gradual forested hillside.

We peered out through the trees and saw the five lakes and the Alaskan Mountain Range, sixty to seventy miles south. In the future, I would be opening this view. There would come a time when I would be sitting in a rocking chair, my rifle at my side, a dog at my feet, and just maybe a wife calling me for supper.

Standing on the house site, I pointed out to Jeff where my lawn, garden, green house, fire wood pile, lumber open-air drying shed, generator building, and the outhouse would be. To Jeff, I was pointing into a forest of tall, fat birch. These trees had been standing for five hundred years, untouched by a forest fire in all that time.

Wildfires have come close at times in the recent past. They likely were here several times in the distance past, centuries and centuries ago. I could see that this location, being just down from the summit, was protected and sheltered from the northwest winds.

The northeast winds would stop the cold winds. Also, it would lessen the fire danger, or at least slow an advancing fire. To add protection, I would clear-cut a fire perimeter and trim the remaining choice trees. I would be removing the undergrowth, along with the dry rotting wood, chewing bug–infested debris.

This would get rid of the mosquito habitat, opening up the area for me to see wild game to shoot as needed, giving me meat conveniently close by.

Alongside this ridge, lower to my west, there was a spot ideal for a garden. This spot had rich soil, nonacidic, made up of hardwoods. It was an area with thousands of years of old growth forest, which would be perfect for making a lawn and garden—after it became cleared and tilled, of course.

The ground gradually slopes, making for good drainage. It has no permafrost and will be exposed to the high daylong sun. This was ideal for growing a garden of anything I wanted, an opportunity to fill a root cellar of canned goods. This would be our sustenance during the long winter nights.

12

Deadly Cold to Warm and Cozy

September 13

Middle of September is the time for the hard freeze, and on this night, we were sleeping in the Eureka tent. It was a long, freezing night, an inspirational night—a night that Jeff will always, before everything else, remember as the night we nearly froze to death.

Our sleeping bags were not rated for freezing temperatures. Like most ratings on boots and sleeping bags, they are always overrated. The general rule is to always get the higher rating.

The night started out cool, but not all that bad. We would be okay once we could zip up our sleeping bags, right? Wrong! Soon we were piling on our light jackets and anything we had.

It was a sleepless, shivering, long, cold night. It grew colder by the hour. I have had many sleepless nights in the past for many reasons, but never for being cold.

The longest night is a night of shivering. When I say shivering, I mean shivering. Shivering is a reflex, a way to keep the body warm, but barely. Just enough to keep us alive is all?

The danger point is when you are no longer shivering and become sleepy. All the while it is cold, even if it is only 54°F. It does not need to be at the freezing point of 32°F.

Without proper clothing, your body's temperature drops below the norm. Your brain starts lying to you, telling you it is warm, or even hot. Hot enough in fact, a person sometimes removes clothing, even at subzero temperatures. This is a comforting, false feeling, where death is the result.

Become aware of that fact before your brain stops reasoning. Test yourself by spelling simple words, common names, or even how the letters *b* and *d* can be used. If that is confusing, get warm. Or in the case of bad air, get to fresh air immediately.

The brain needs to be warm, and it needs safe, breathable air. Without clean air, it can result in carbon dioxide poisoning. If it is the carbon dioxide problem, you will know it by the headache that immediately follows after breathing good air. Carbon dioxide, mixed in with good air, is caused by several things. Educate yourself and others.

Sunrise was the deciding factor. It is the coldest hour of the twenty-four hours, at dawn's first light. Jeff had a solid, small pool of ice outside, near the foot end of his sleeping bag. We had to get up to warm ourselves by exercising, and then built a campfire.

We needed to run in place before we could even hold a match to light our campfire. Our fingers and bodies were shaking too much to hold a match, let alone strike it.

Once we got a roaring fire, we toasted our bodies like they were hot dogs. We were dancing around the fire and feeding the Fire God lots of wood, chanting, "We shall live!" Right after, we had a breakfast of hot pancakes.

All that day, it rained leaves, a confirming sign of a hard freeze. By nightfall, the trees were barren. Winter would be here any day with snow. In Alaska, there is no spring or fall, only summers and winters. Commonly, springs and falls are no longer than a few fleeting days.

The inspirational part from this freezing night was when my brain was activated like I was the chairman of the board of the largest corporation in the world. My brain took charge; it was like I had pushed the chair away from the head of the oval table with the board members looking at me.

I quickly stood up, leaned over, and pounded the conference table hard with my clinched closed fists. This made the water glasses and the glass ashtrays rise up revolving, dancing, and spiraling.

Finally, the ashtrays came back to a stop, capturing the attention of the board members. Before the water glasses and glass ashtrays had come to a stop, I said, "Tonight by golly, we will be warm!"

I must have spoken out loud, for Jeff said, "What did you say?"

"I said, tonight we will be warm!"

Without any explanation or discussion, I told Jeff to empty his backpack and go down to base camp. I asked him to bring back the disposable wood stove, the chimney pipes, the roll of black poly, and the shovel. "I will be busy here with the chainsaw. Tonight we will be inside a warm lean-to."

"Okay, that sounds good to me." Off he went.

My thought was, *Thank goodness for young men.*

Jeff went on his way to base camp. My plan was to build the framework for a lean-to large enough for our supplies. It would have a wood stove for heat and be available for us eat and sleep in while we would build.

My plan was to build a small, log trapper's cabin, in the days to come. It would also serve as a habitable dwelling requirement for proving up my homestead.

I needed a steep hillside for this lean-to and found it near the tent. It was down, to the east of the ridgeline. This steep slope had a thick stand of black spruce, on which to hang, or support, a lean-to frame. This shelter would not be small. I liked my space and wanted no more tenting. Winter was upon us.

I have had all sorts of building experiences. This ranged from building tree houses as a kid, tunneling in snow and sand, to building a five-man heated machine gun bunker on the Demilitarized Zone (DMZ) in South Korea, and later, in the building of apartment complexes, townhouses, and small single family rambler homes.

I have also had experience in the rocks (granite stone quarries) located in the Minnesota River Valley, enlarging a stone cave by exploding and cleaving large parts of the frozen stone walls. I did this in the subzero cold winter, with a huge bonfire, making it livable within hours.

That was followed by removing the busted cleaved off stone and building an eleven-man lean-to on one of my parents woodlots—the one on the high bluff, made from the melting ice age river Warren, known today as the Minnesota River and its valley. There would be no problem in building a lean-to in the wilderness of Alaska.

There was no need to make posts or dig the holes for them. I found standing, live trees for the corners and one tree in the center of the upper end of the support frame. The two lower corner trees were anywhere from six to eight inches in diameter.

I trimmed the trees of their branches as high as I could reach with the chainsaw and then supported myself up high on a makeshift log stand at the base of these two trees. I eye-leveled and sawed off the trees at eight or so feet above the ground, making the tops flat.

The back two corners, up higher on the hillside, I eye-leveled them too, keeping them even with the two front ones, topping them flat as well.

On the upper center tree that was in line with the two upper tree posts, I just trimmed the branches off as high as I could. Then let the tree stand for the time being. The four corners were an area of 12' × 10' apart, parallel and leveling with the hillside, and formed a near perfect rectangle.

Next, I needed two long logs to top the two twelve-foot spans. I would be leaving extra lengths for them to extend beyond the high end of the tree-rooted posts. I sawed one more log that would be round notched, to fit across the ten-foot span. One end of the longer log would be placed first on the high end of the corner tree support post.

After I had cut those lengths, I cleared the smaller trees and bush from the center area. This way we would be able to move about without stumbling.

I heard a stomping noise on the ridge, back above me. It was Jeff. No wonder there was a stomping noise; he was carrying a heavier load than he weighed.

Looking at Jeff reminded me of the time I spent in South Korea, seeing what those civilians could carry on their backs. Jeff was hunched over too, by balancing a ton on his back, with his hands full as well.

He had brought back up the hill of three and a half miles what I had requested, and more. He was a human mule. On his back was tied the stove, the heavy roll of black poly, his stuffed full backpack, and the things hanging off of that.

"*My Lord, Jeff,*" I said. I then helped him unload, handing him a canteen of water.

"I brought up that box of twelve-inch bridge spikes we got from Mark Weronko too, thought we'd need them sooner or later. Plus, I brought the two-pound ball ball-peen hammer."

"*Wow!* Jeff, that box alone is all of twenty-five pounds. Rest, and later you can help me place some logs for the frame."

Jeff then replied, "I am fine."

With that, we went to placing the three logs and spiking them on top of the tree posts. Next, the ridgepole (center beam) was selected. Before placing that, the top end tree had to be dropped to support the ridgepole on its top, on down to the cross log at the lower end.

This, too, was only eyeballed. As was the center, top-end tree post. After all, this was only a lean-to; it did not need to be perfect. It was wise to have the ridgepole higher than the sides for drainage.

While saying this, I remember the time on a job site in Savage, Minnesota. I was helping build a horse barn for the race horses. There was something the boss of mine at the time once said, after he overheard an employee. "It's only a horse barn. I don't know why it has to be perfect."

The boss just happened to be walking by and responded in a loud tone with a gruff voice, "It might be only a horse barn, but it will be the best damn horse barn anywhere." That block layer almost lost his job. I guess I learned something that day, and it stuck with me ever since. To be the best you're able, taking pride in all that you do.

The lean-to frame was almost ready to cover with the poly sheeting. Snow would be falling soon. The poly roof would need to be supported for the snow load, and additionally, the moss that would cover the poly for retaining the heat.

The rafters would be simple. Short lengths, by eight inch in diameter birch logs, not of spruce. Spruce would have been prickly, punching holes in the poly, and making for a leaky roof. Nothing fancy, time was short. Each log was placed interlocking, like folded, church-praying fingers.

It would have a six-inch overhang on the sides, to just past the ridgepole center. I was busy dropping the trees, cutting them into the necessary lengths roughly, to be trimmed after they were placed. Jeff was laying them up in place, not nailing or notching, just laying them up.

They did not need to be nailed or notched. The space between each was as wide as each of the logs, but fairly evenly spaced. It was not long before Jeff reported we had enough.

With my chainsaw, I trimmed the overhang, flatting the logs to six inches. They were smooth cut in order to nail a smooth smaller log, for the poly to be draped over the edges. The poly would then be extending down to the ground.

Jeff went and nailed up the overhang trim log. Meanwhile, I went on top and trimmed the log top's overlapping ends, which were protruding up above the other logs on the ridge pole. I smoothed them of all the sharp ends. The roof had a nice low crown, which would be good enough for drainage.

Next, Jeff had a five-gallon gasoline can cut and ready for the chimney pipe. It would be placed through the roof to fireproof it. We picked out a likely place for the stove to be, and above that, I nailed the chimney can between two roof logs. This chimney metal can would keep the heat from transferring to a combustible surface.

"Okay! We're ready to cover it and move in." Jeff dug out a temporary platform for the wood stove on the side hill inside, and then installed the chimney pipe. We cut up a bunch of handy firewood, and we were warm that night.

Mind you, this was a steep hillside, so after supper, Jeff dug out some bunks to sleep on. That first night, Jeff explained to me while being warm and cozy, "When you said a lean-to, I was thinking of a pole propped up to a tree for a small lean-to, but, man! This is colossal!"

"Now you know what the shovel is for, Jeff. Tomorrow, you can dig more space out, filling the buckets, and I will toss the dirt on the top to shape. I will be taking out the weeps and sags, in order to form a smooth, watershed, sloping roof. That way, we won't have any wet, muddy places that leak. Rather, the bulk of the water drains off, saving enough of the water in the moss to keep the roof alive.

Over this now smooth, formed earthen roof, more poly sheeting would be placed. Then it would then be covered with six to eight inches of moss, for insulation.

"Where did you learn all this, Duane?"

"Prior experience, Jeff. Experience goes a long way." During some point that night of talking, we fell fast asleep.

13

Transitioning Time

"How did you sleep, Jeff?"

"Fantastic."

"Me too," I said.

After breakfast, Jeff began to remove the dirt while I gathered a pile of ground moss and stacked it up close to the lean-to. There was no problem in gathering moss from this very old forest floor. In places, the moss was two feet thick.

Together, we began to toss the dirt on the roof. We spread it around, being sure there were no sags or dips. We didn't need much dirt, just enough to shape it for drainage.

When we had finished with that, the next poly sheeting was placed on, and the sides were secured. To be sure, we placed a second sheet of poly on top of that one. We tossed up on those eight inches of ground moss.

"Good thing we got the moss when we did. It sure does feel like it could snow. The ground moss will be all covered one of these days soon," Jeff said.

"It sure looks that way, Jeff. I best get at the building of the trapper's cabin. Perhaps you can keep on trucking up the supplies. There is no telling how deep the snow will get on that trail once it snows."

Jeff went about the daunting task of carrying up every item we had at base camp, over the next few days. He brought up the three different packs we had. One was a hard backpack board that was left there by the Frenchman Bernard. It came in real handy for strapping on the portable generator, which was very awkward for one person to carry.

Also, he brought up the remaining five-gallon gasoline cans, weighing thirty-five pounds each. In one of those hauling trips, Jeff brought up four full, five-gallon gasoline cans. Unbelievable! It had to have been his biggest, heaviest trip of all. I think he carried a rifle then too.

One trip had gallons of chainsaw bar oil and mix oil. Another had a twelve-volt car battery that had to be carried without tipping it. Later, in other trips, he brought up the cases of food and as much of the drinking water as possible in five-gallon water containers. I think the last thing Jeff brought up was the generator.

About the water supply, I had made a hillside water catch pond out of black poly sheeting early on. I did that on the first day we got up there, and luckily too. It rained, filling it that night. It froze solid the next night, but we then had ice to melt.

No snow had fallen yet. There was a flowing spring downhill about eight hundred feet, but we did not need it. It was a steep hill, so it was easier to collect rain, or melt snow for water.

For communicating, we used our car dashboard CB, with its antenna at base camp. Our handheld CB on the hill was used at appointed times to check in on each other. Jeff would be packing things to haul up, then he would get some rest before he would finish coming back up, fully loaded.

There was one day Jeff stayed up on the hill. I went on down with the chainsaw to trim some taller stumps. Since the moss had been trumped down some, the stumps needed to be leveled to the hard ground. Plus, hanging into the trail were some small trees that should be removed before the snow.

I also felt this should be done before the next year's adventure with an ATV. I did not think there would be much involved. A full tank of gasoline in the chainsaw should do the trick. I was planning to be back before dark and before Jeff's supper.

Well, so much for that plan. I had plenty of gasoline, or at least enough. What I did not plan for was the time it took to do this. I was not going to do this again, so I kept on working. I finished before dark and was planning on staying the night at base camp. I called Jeff on the CB from there, to let him know.

When I called Jeff, I told him it was too late for me to be back tonight. I would need more light to make a safe trip on that stubbly, newly cut trail, and I did not need his help. I heard Jeff say good-night, and then he hung up.

What I did not know was that Jeff had heard me say, "I need help," instead of the words "I do not need help."

Jeff replied, "Are you alright?" Not the word "goodnight," which I had heard. After that, the CB went dead. Neither of us realizing some of the batteries were low.

I was fixing the bunk to lie down, when the door opened. In popped Jeff! "What is wrong?" Jeff asked, as he was out of breath.

I was in shock and replied, "Nothing! What the heck are you doing here? I just was talking to you eight minutes ago."

Jeff had run down that three-and-a-half-mile trail, stumbling over newly cut trees. Running as fast as he could, in the darkness, he did this without stopping, or stumbling. Better yet, not breaking or twisting an ankle, running to my aid.

Jeff and I both ended up spending the night at base camp and would make our trip back up to the lean-to in the morning. The Frenchman's cabin once again saved the day, in this case, the night.

14

Change of Plans

To make it a habitable dwelling, our lodging would be a small trapper's cabin built from logs. This trapper's cabin site was not being built on the spot where the real home would be built. Rather, it was to be way back, and higher up on the ridge. It would be located off to the side of the game trail, just above the lean-to and close to the tent. That way it would not interfere with the bigger projects, which would come later. It was, however, still near the trail.

Building a cabin of logs is a very common thing that many people dream of doing. Many do, much the same as I was.

Winter was coming on fast, so I had to get the post holes dug before the ground would freeze. I needed the poles placed so I could begin laying up the four walls. Knowing that wood logs left on the ground will rot, it is best to build a cabin above the ground. Having no stone to build the foundation, I had no other choice.

In order to retain the heat inside the cabin, the logs would have to be large in diameter. This is why I decided on a small cabin. Green large logs are heavy. Small in diameter logs would make for a cold cabin.

The floor would have to be heavily insulated as well, even more than the roof. Having a warm lean-to would be a very big help in getting the cabin built since it was so late in the year. Coming to the realization of the limited time that we had left to accomplish what all we needed to was a wake-up call for me.

We had been working on this cabin for two days. During that second night after supper in the warm cozy lean-to, I announced that I had a change of plans.

"Jeff! I am scrapping the trapper's cabin project, and this will be the dwelling."

Jeff replied, "Here in the lean-to?"

"Yup, right here. Only, instead of a lean-to, it will become a dugout. We will live in it while we build it. We have big birch trees for the lumber logs and a chainsaw mill to saw the lumber."

"During the day, you dig and I will mill the lumber. At night, we will nail up the boards on the outer walls. As you excavate the inside, the inside walls will be nailed. First, I will make boards for the building of an outhouse. I like my comfort when it comes to going to the bathroom."

The next morning, I picked out a location that had three standing trees, in order to be used for the corners of the outhouse frame. The fourth corner would have to be a free post. It would just be set into the solid ground, and this would be attached to the others.

One nearby spruce tree would be used as a ladder to complete the roof. Jeff dug the pit five feet deep, going through three layers of frost from the years past. Each day that he hit a layer of frost, he would wait a day for it to thaw. He would continue to dig more the next day. He continued this through three layers of frost.

Each layer was at a different depth, depending on the insulating snow cover of that year's winter. It was not permafrost, but annual frosts. Jeff did not find much for rocks, finding only a few hunks of quartz rock.

As Jeff was doing one thing or another, I was busy falling birch and making lumber. This important building (outhouse) was about eighty feet away from the site for the lean-to, and slightly sloping downhill to the east. Its door would face east, overlooking the rim of a large tree forest in a box canyon, with its outlet to the south.

This outhouse, being on sloping ground with the door facing downhill, would become a raised outhouse. It would need a stairway to get to the door and the bench seat. We used smaller spruce logs for framing the stairs, on which the two-inch-thick planks for the steps would be nailed.

The outside wall boards would be overlapping by one-half inch or more to keep the rain and wind out, like the siding boards are on a house. Two-inch planks were used for the flooring and bench.

The outhouse was raised on one side because it was placed on a hill. The side where the door was located was the side that was higher from the ground. These meant steps would be required.

For the building of the stairway, I used two long, round logs for the stringers. Stringers are what support the steps. Each step was made from a plank cut to two inches thick, by eleven inches wide, and three feet long. These flat steps were supported by smaller-sized logs, which ran from stringer to stringer. These short supporting logs were placed down before the steps were nailed onto them. This made for a safe and solid stairway, with a hand railing off to one side for support.

September 26

This day, we made the frame as well as some planks, and it snowed, covering the ground. The outhouse was usable before completion. I was busy sawing the 3/4-inch thick boards.

Jeff nailed them on in the afternoons; earlier in the day, he finished bringing up the supplies from base camp. Also, he would hunt for supper and, in general, explore.

I was a lumber-sawing fool. That is about all I did, except for the times I ran the camcorder, recording this building in this wilderness experience.

The previous day, Jeff had severely slashed his hand with a sharp double bit ax while splitting kindling wood early in the morning. This happened before I was awake.

I taped it up best I could, closing the cut together with butterfly medical tape (pulling the wound close). That way, it would heal closed. The taping looked bad, like he wore a half of a glove with his bare fingers exposed. It was his favored left hand too.

For some reason, he did not let me sew up his big bad open wound. Nor would he let me dump gunpowder in the wound to cauterize it. It would have hurt like heck for only a moment, but nope. He would have nothing to do with that.

I guess maybe having no whiskey for him to get drunk on was a big factor. I was able to convince him I had to pour bleach on it, or it would have become infected. That was hard for him too. He took it like the man he had become.

September 29

Jeff completed the roof of the outhouse with his newly wrapped up hand.

15

Building of the Dugout

October 4

We had our first heavy snowfall; it snowed all day. The outer walls of the dugout were completed, even in a heavy snowfall. No door yet though, only poly sheeting for a door. The door was yet to be made.

Excavating on a hillside has the advantage of only needing to remove the dirt out of the dugout, leveling the floor space, and relocating the dirt over the edge of the hill, followed by leveling and extending the front outside area of the dugout.

Dugouts are something that was done in the past by our forefathers. The houses they built are also called sod houses. I am glad to be a part of living history physically, not only through reading about how they did things to survive. Those early pioneers out on the prairies made their first homes of blocks of sod. The resulting dugouts were very energy efficient. I highly respect our ancestors' abilities.

The digging posed no problem, for it was all made of volcanic ash that had drifted into place. The ash conformed to and covered the stone base under the surface of the ridge and the hill. The land under the ash in this area was first formed by rock.

The hardest part was the chopping of the ground covers, the roots, and stumps. Because there was no rock, the ax blade seldom became dull. The compaction of this ash was firm and freestanding. It was easily shaped to make the walls plumb, with no sloughing or caving in.

The board walls were made in two parts, after the roof and corners were first constructed. Mind you, we lived in this as it was being built, so we had to take a different approach in the construction of the walls. It was winter, and Mother Nature is the mother of innovation.

Before the bulk of the soil was removed, save for the space required for our immediate needs, the outer wall posts were installed two feet apart. Each was of a different height under the log wall beams. We placed the wall posts one by one resting on the sloping hillside, after the moss had been removed.

The wall posts were simple, six-inch-diameter spruce logs. The poly sheeting that had been draped over the outside was now covered by 3/4" thick boards and nailed to these spruce posts in a shiplap fashion, the siding overlapping each other by 1½", in the same way the boards on the outhouse were done.

We had a close call while slicing the dirt on the back wall to embed the posts for the inner wall boards. We had a near cave-in. I had become too complacent about digging because the soil had been showing no signs of caving in and appeared stable.

I had forgot about the possibility of a sloughing of the dirt in the walls that were straight up and down, before we had the hardened board walls up. All was going well, but remember that supporting tree in the back, the center ridgepole support?

I had forgotten how close it was to the excavated edge, and with the addition of the wood timbers and moss on the top adding extra weight. If it had been only a post, and not a root-based tree, it would have not have given me any warning. It would have caved right on down on us, bringing down the roof.

There was a small slide of earth, a slight movement. Not of the ridgepole, just the dirt under the base of the tree that was the support of the center roof pole, called the ridgepole.

Either by fate, or luck, we were both working in there when this happened. Boy! I kid you not. Jeff and I were a working team then. We ran out and quickly sawed down a six- to eight-inch diameter spruce tree of sufficient length.

Jeff, with the drawknife, skinned it before placing it as a supporting post. In a short time, we had that post placed tight under the ridgepole, near the back wall. Just far enough from the dirt wall to have room for the wood wall that had yet to be built. We made sure to leave enough room for the bunks.

This post was now tight under the ridgepole, and on the solid dirt floor. Jeff had hurriedly removed the loose earth that had fallen on the smooth floor, in order to place the post. This quick action stopped any further caving in and gave the proper support the ridgepole needed.

When the excavation inside was complete, and the outer walls were in place, the wall posts from the dirt floor to the existing upper sloping wall posts were placed and spliced. We only removed the earthen soil channels for the length and widths of the posts.

Embedding the posts in the earth walls made for no fill needed, or settling. An entire wall sheet of poly was tacked on the inside, on the full-length wall posts. We left enough on the bottom to lap the sheeting with that, which was on the dirt floor for about a foot. The board walls were nailed on from the floor up, horizontally.

As the inside boards rose above the earth hillside, they were nailed. It was then that we used moss to fill into the space of the empty wall, between the poly's lined, boarded walls. No moss was needed behind the portion of the earthen lower walls, which were backed by the original soil.

Only the poly vapor barrier and the two-foot center posts were needed. This was followed by the wood boards. The poly sheeting would keep the wood walls dry and free of mold. When no air reaches wood under the surface, and just below the surface, the wood will last almost indefinitely.

Rotting only occurs above the surface and just below the surface, much like wooden fence posts in a pasture. Keeping it airtight and dry extends the life of a wood post. So these walls will last almost forever.

Next, it was time for the wood flooring. Small log stringers were embedded in the earth floor, two feet on center, and leveled flush to the earth floor. There would be a poly vapor barrier over them, covering the floor and overlapping the extensions of the wall vapor barriers. The extended poly sheeting was extending onto the floor. This overlapping made the floor water tight and dry.

One-inch-thick and wider boards were nailed down to the embedded floor joists. This is the same way I placed a concrete basement floor for a dry usable floor, which is then good for laying tile on, or painting. Concrete alone does not stop water or dampness. It needs to have poly uncut sheeting beneath the concrete and, in this case, under a wood flooring.

Inside the dugout, before the wood floor was placed, the soil had to be regularly dampened in order to keep the dust down. The heat from the woodstove lifted the fine dust up with the waves of heat. This soil was not regular black heavy dirt. This soil was made of volcanic ash that was easily sucked up with the heat rising from the stove. In the old sod days, earth wet tamped floors were common. They would become like concrete due to the heavier soils.

We finished placing the larger, one-inch-thick by one-foot-wide boards. These were cut to full length and width of the room, which now had an inside dimension of nine feet wide, wall to wall, and eleven feet long. We were now dust free.

It was now time to build other things like shelves, a table, a double rope bunk, benches, and a raised fireproof stand for the woodstove. This raised fireproof support stand saved us from bending over to load it and added ease of cooking on it.

October 5

According to my design, Jeff began to work on making the double rope bunk frame. It was made from spruce logs, bunks being one lower bed, and one higher. The pole frames would be strongly made to hold a webbing of 1/4" hemp rope.

It would have two inches on center, tautly crossed. It would be checked laced over under each rope, crossing between the frame ends and sides. This would make a sleeping space of seven feet by three feet. Each of the two long lengths of ropes per bunk, made to be adjustable in the tensions, for the best comfort zone at any time.

Each of the four uprights, in order to support the two bunks, had to have two 1½" bored holes and located at the right measured places. On each end of a bunk frame, the short log ends of the bunks would look like a spud axle. The log ends would be the same size as the bored holes in the uprights. These axles would be long enough to be inserted into the uprights, or the post's bored holes.

The long posts of each horizontal bunk would be flushed and counter sunk, locked to fit tight. A 12" x 3/8" bridge spike would be spiked through the thick logs of the spud axles and into the ends of the long posts of the bunk frames. After the two bunks are installed on the legs, the spud axles would be locked in place by a small nail on each of the eight axle ends (two bunks). This limited any movement and could then be disassembled at will.

The bunk frames (logs) would have half-inch holes drilled through the logs on all four sides, spaced apart two inches on their center of the horizontal poles. Through these holes, the quarter-inch rope would be threaded from hole to hole, not over or under the frame. Rope webbing was used versus wood, for the comfort and nesting. I had found and salvaged a large spool of quarter-inch hemp rope from an abandoned cabin, which was never proved up.

The lower bunk would be at bench seat height, or knee-high. The top bunk would be high enough to keep you from hitting the pole frame with your head while sitting on the bottom bunk edge. However, if we were to stand up straight without first leaning forward, it would not be good.

Having a 9'6" ceiling made good sense in many ways; this double bunk was but one reason to have a high ceiling. To climb up to the top bunk, a 1½" wood dowel peg system was staggered to climb on the one upright pole at the wall end of the bunk. Below the bottom bunk was the storage space for the five-gallon bucket containers, which would be then out of the way.

During the draw-knifing of this rope bunk building, Jeff had a mishap. There was a stub that was being stubborn in being smoothed with the big log draw-knifed. With some great force, he pulled it hard, and it sliced the stub smooth.

In the process, the blade of this sharp big log draw knife cut deep into his kneecap, all the way to the bone. Again, I was a doctor. I patched him up. For days after that, Jeff had a stiff knee, but it did not slow him down.

I have asked Jeff to make a chapter for this book telling of his adventures, personal accounts, and feelings. Jeff wrote a poem for this book too. I gave it the title "Reminisces," by Jeff Peterson. I have also placed in the front of this book some mighty fine words Jeff wrote that I will forever be grateful for. Thank you ever so much, Jeff. You make me proud to have you as a friend.

October 6

The portable generator was placed in the outhouse beside the toilet seat, where there was room for it. There was space for more shelving, higher up on the sides. We hung high, safe from bears and moose, the electric extension cord on trees to the dugout.

This was for the use of charging the car battery, lights, and camcorder batteries. A volt meter was attached to the 12-volt battery to show us when we needed to charge the battery. That was usually done nightly.

What kills the lifespan of a battery is running it down to zero often and charging it back up. This shortens the life of a battery, and it will not be working for the expected five-year life, and often longer.

Keep the battery at 12.3 volts at all times, even though the battery indicates it is at 12 volts, which does not mean it is full of storage amps, or in peak condition. Putting a load tester on the battery will show how healthy it is.

Here's another tidbit of story that I find interesting. That night, Jeff built a two-place, small kitchen table for us to eat from. What made this table special is that Jeff made it without using nails. He made it all with drilled holes and wood pegs. Jeff drilled the holes with the wood brace and a set of wood drill bits.

I had brought these tools all the way up from New Ulm, Minnesota. I had bought them there at an antique store. I also purchased other old usable things from this store for this wilderness experience.

The wood pegs he made were of dry wood. They were bound tight by a wedge in the center of the pegs, with a dab of spruce pitch for glue. The table is still in the dugout and used today.

The raised box stand for the wood heat stove served two purposes. First, it was at a height for convenience. Second, it kept the heat from transferring to the flammable wood floor, or its stand.

The stand was covered with tin, having a one-and-a-half-inch airspace between the box, and the table cross-boarded top. It was also covered with tin; the one-and-a-half-inch space between was supported on four wood dowel pins. The tinned, cross-boarded top is where the stove was secured. Elaborate, I know, but it was done to our specs.

The last thing to be built was the door. I had made the door opening early on to have a four-foot-wide door. Why four feet? I wanted a wide door to drive ATVs or a snow machine inside, in order to store, and/or work on. This also warmed up the machines in order to get them started in subzero temps.

This is called thinking ahead. In Alaska, it is never safe to leave anything outside where bears can destroy it. All my buildings would have doors wide enough to bring in all my equipment, for all those reasons.

Bears break in some cabins by pulling apart the corner logs, or caving in a door by bouncing on it. If they find any give, anywhere, they will continue to bounce on it until it falls away. Once inside, they will make a mess finding another way to get out, busting through a second door or window.

A cabin owner might be able to shoot a vandal to eat, but first, you have to be there with a gun in hand. So never leave anything out for the bear or wolverine. While you're inside, you are always alert to any noises, and a heavy weapon is handy. It's not prudent to leave your weapon on the rack with the bullets in a drawer.

Rather, you want a big gun that is loaded, with the safety on, placed by the door or aside your chair. This is where a dog would be handy to have for companionship, as well as a guard.

This door was inner framed with an X-bracing, in order to be rigid. This framework was made to be insulated and strong. It had a triple paned Plexiglas, for frost-free viewing. Also, it would be a warm window, keeping in the heat, and the cold out.

The window, which was 3' × 3', was also removable from the inside. This was in case of needing to fire a weapon from the open window, without alerting whatever you might need to kill.

The building of this window frame had to include being measured properly. It had to be marked to have each pane a quarter inch apart, to have airspace insulating the window from frosting and losing heat. This would keep it from letting in the cold through the panes.

The 12 cuts (four sides) for the three panes were made 3/8" deep by 1/8" wide. This made for a close fit, plus allowed for the expansion and contraction of the three panes during the temperature changes. The frame was cut with the four edges of spruce, a softwood dimensional lumber, of 2" × 1½" of half-lapped corners (not butted). They would be nailed after the three panes were embedded a quarter inch into the four edges of the wooden, dissembled frame.

I had no skill saw, or a radial arm saw, to make the cuts easy for this triple-pane window. The chainsaw cut would have been too wide for the window panes to fit tightly for sealing. Each pane needed to be able to have just enough room to be able to expand and contract, as the temperatures changed. If there was not enough room, the panes would crack.

For this, I used my try square, a chainsaw round file, and my two-foot framing square. I didn't use a saw. On each inner edge of the disassembled frame, I measured with the two-foot framing square, drawing out the twelve lines in total on the frame.

Three lines on each frame side, of all three panes, of course making sure the alignments were correct. I centered the three lines from the center out, allowing airspace between each pane of a quarter inch. This made for a warm, frost-free window, once assembled.

With the lines now drawn, I laid the square flat along a line to be cut. I cut one line at a time, using that line in aiding me to use the square as a solid guide, when cutting or grooving each of the twelve cuts.

The adjustable try square was used to make the cuts, much as a block plane. First, I had to use that round file to make a cutting tooth on the one end of the sliding, grooved, one-foot steel ruler. The tooth was made like a chainsaw tooth.

I made a relief behind this tooth so I could set the depth of each cut. I used the set screw to relock the ruler, or what was now the cutter, each time. The body of the try square has a flat edge; this rested on the wood. Alongside this body, the framing square was used to press against it like a backstop, as I pushed the cutter along on the line drawn.

After each pass was made, I lowered the cutting tooth deeper. This one-foot ruler was the perfect thickness, the same thickness as the panes. As the cut became deep enough, the framing square was no longer needed. Each pass, the cutter was lowered only slightly.

The grooving was finished after each groove reached the 3/8" depth mark, 1/8" deeper than the pane's edge, which would be fitting in the finished frame. This allowed for the panes to move, seeing how the grooves were cut deeper than the size of the pane. Cutting the twelve grooves for the three panes was a long, arduous, enduring job, but well worth the time.

I now had a warm window to look out of. The wooden frame was half lapped at the ends on the four corners, and nailed tight. This window is removable, and still in full working order today.

The hollow door, save for the interiors X-bracing, was sealed with poly sheeting on both inner faces and filled with fine dry moss. It was boarded on both the inside and outside, next to the three massive wood hinges needed to be built.

Each night while I slept, I planned for the next project that was to be done the following day. I do think I work harder in my sleep than when I am awake, but this saves me time. At times, when I cannot completely see in my dreams the answer, the answer comes to me while I am doing it.

These three wooden hinges were made of dry, dead spruce. The wood had been heated to harden. The hinges had to be made strong for this solid heavy door, which was built of green birch lumber. The hinges needed to be massive in order to carry the door's weight. Each part of the three hinges attached across the door would be five feet in length, five inches wide, and four inches thick.

The hinge sections would be in six parts for the three hinges, one part of each hinge would attach to the wall, the other part to the door. There would be an upper hinge above the long door hinge end; the second wall hinge would be under the door hinge. Each wall hinge would be three feet long by five inches wide and four inches thick.

These three hinges called for 15-inch dowel pins, each 1½" in diameter. The 1½" holes had to be perfectly in line for the hinge to operate correctly. A jig was made for this, so all holes were bored the same and were square in two directions, or inline. The holes were made by an old-fashion hand auger. Jeff had the honors to bore the holes under my watchful eye.

Before the hinges could be attached, the heavy door was set in place in the door opening, temporally securing it. The bottom of the door was shimmed upward for relief, and it gave it room to settle for a finer fit once the door was operational.

The hinges were made correctly, but they now had to be attached correctly. This meant squaring the door frame. Where the door would be hinged, the door and frame had to be marked exact before the hinges could be attached. Since the hinges were longer than normal, they had to be perfect.

Proper measuring was done to make the three doweled holes in the right place. We checked three times before bridge spiking the door hinges permanently to the door. With heavy grease, we greased the 15-inch dowels one by one and installed them in the three parts of each hinge. They were bridge spiked permanently to the wall. We then removed the shims from under the door, releasing the temporarily secured door, and prayed.

Jeff watched as I slowly opened the door. *Creak! Moan! Groan!* The dowels were squeaking, but it worked! No binding at all, and no hesitation. The door worked like a charm, perfectly level, and not falling away or falling closed. Rather, it stayed where it was placed.

It was time to add on the door latch, handles, trick door lock, and the weather stripping to seal the door airtight.

Since I had forgotten to buy a door latch, I was faced with making one. Anyway, this door was of vault size. No regular doorknob would do unless it was a push-pull freezer door, like the doors in a meat locker found in butcher shops.

It was time to be inventive again. Handles can be made out of oddly shaped roots or tree limbs. With my chainsaw, I made, on the inside of the dugout door, a rectangular latch block to lock the door. I used gravity for a wooden toggle bar that loosely fit but was snug in the latch block (see photo). The toggle bar could be raised or dropped into a groove of the frame of the door. This latching block was attached at doorknob height on the inside of the dugout.

The old latches of the 1800s were not in the door but on the door. I bored a hole through the door and above the latch block for a 3/8" diameter bridge spike to loosely slide through, by pulling or pushing. Outside, the pointed end of the spike would be bent downward. A wooden handle with a 3/8" × 3" bored a hole, in at one end, on which to wedge the bent spike for a wood gripped handle.

On the bridge spike head above the door latch, I tied a doubled leather shoestring. It was doubled for extra security. The shoestring would hang down to the wooden, pivoting, gravity falling, 8" × 1" latch. When that latch was lowered, it would loosely fit into the recess for the wooden latch block.

The latch, in turn, was freely pegged by a 1/2" dowel that was placed through the block, passing through the fixed pivoting end of the latch. The latch, when leveled and closed, fitted in a recessed groove on the wall frame of the door. Thus, the door was then latched closed.

To open this door from the inside, you pushed the spike into the door. From the outside to open the door, you pulled the wood-covered spike.

Now for the trick door lock. There would be no metal hasp or padlocks to lock the door. I was reminded in a dream of how I did it in my past life as an Egyptian. Trick doors were common then.

One trick, I remembered, involved having a torch on the wall. When it was raised or pulled down, a secret door opened. Okay, then why not a decorative birch burl in the wall up high, within easy reach, and made to look like it was there as a decorative thing, useful only to look at.

I made a trick door locking mechanism, much in the same manner as the trick doors for the hidden chambers in the Egyptian pyramids. For my door, I used the wooden burl. This burl was the key to unlocking the door.

Completing the trick door locking mechanism made this dugout a habitable dwelling, which was now complete. Mission accomplished. It was November 9, 1986.

16

Outtakes

While we were building, sawing lumber, and living in this dugout, we had a few other things going on that I should mention. I call this chapter "Outtakes."

The AM and FM radio reception was vastly better up here than it was down below at base camp. Up high on the hill, we had several stations to listen to. No big deal right? Well, we had spent a few months in the wilderness, far from radio stations that were often blocked by terrain.

The reception was particularly bad in the bottomlands, so it was especially good to hear some other voices, besides the ones in your head and the ones in your dreams. The key, as I mentioned before early on, is to keep busy in getting adjusted to the solitude and the silence; there was a lack of mankind's noises, realizing you're not in Kansas anymore.

This could hold true even being within a crowd and having the noise of people all around. I have known this feeling in a crowd. It is the worst kind of alone. To be in a crowd, not being able to fit in, or even wanting to.

I guess that is due to being different. After time, being in the wilderness is more of a comfort than being in the so-called civilized world, which I call the "rat race of man."

There comes a time when everyone needs rest or a change of routine. Neither Jeff nor I were ever bored. The music, songs sung, news from the outside, letters from home, comradery, observing nature's wonders, and the feeding of the wildlife had made us whole.

In Alaska, the jays are not blue. Rather, they are gray. We have two different types of squirrels, pine and the flying night squirrels. The flying night squirrels, which don't fly but actually glide, have big eyes.

The flying squirrels are out in the lowest twilight hours of the summer, as well as during the long dark nights of winter. We fed a single pine squirrel daily and several gray jays from the dugout. They provided us with entertainment for hours and hours.

Both of us could feed the jays from our mouths. The jays had no fear at all. The squirrel would come close but was more interested in fending off the jays and hogging all the food for himself. Jeff and I had our daily morning pancakes but always had extra to share.

Jeff left a pile of soil to the right front of the poly-covered door opening, and this is where we placed the food. On this pile, we placed a whole, pan-sized pancake for them to eat or pack away. That was the first and only day we did it like that. The greedy squirrel would fold it up and trot off with it, tripping on it as he ran.

The next day, I drove a 12-inch bridge spike partway into the top of this pile of soil. We placed a pancake down onto the spike. This made the squirrel a bit mad, or maybe it was puzzled. He tried everything to carry it off in one piece. The spike part was too high for him to lift it off, so he gave up that idea.

The squirrel even tried to chew the nail but soon gave that up. Then he would bite and lift an edge of the pancake. Running around the spike with the pancake in his mouth, he would go one full circle stop, and then go back the other way, getting nowhere, and looking confused. Again, he stood back with a puzzled look on his face.

About that time, Jeff said to me, "I don't think he likes you for doing that." We were watching and filming him from the warmth of the dugout, through the poly door opening. He and the jays ended up taking bits at a time that day.

One time Jeff put a pancake on the spike hot, right off the frying pan. The squirrel came right in and bit it. Quickly, he backed off. With his front right paw, the squirrel swept snow on it, running all around the pancake. He slapped snow on the pancake as fast as he could run around it.

He knew how to cool it off without even a moment's thought. That was amazing to us. This had to have been his first and only experience, eating anything hot. This squirrel did not just get dropped off a turnip truck. He was no dummy.

The squirrel had to learn to be content with taking small mouth-sized pieces, running off to hide them somewhere. The jays would come next, to peck away on what was left behind as fast as they could, before the squirrel would return. The squirrel would panicky, wildly, and madly come running back to chase the jays away.

The jays figured out a new attack system. They would dive-bomb the squirrel, making him duck, until he got tired of being buzzed by them. He would then take after the bird that buzzed him. The plan was working for the jays. The squirrel was rapidly, and angrily, chasing the birds from tree to tree. He would jump after the birds from branch to branch, nearly catching the jays at times.

This dive-bombing bird would lead the squirrel as far away in a straight line as possible, away from the pancake. This well-coordinated plan was a success. The other jays would then come in and have their fill, quickly eating, packing it away.

The jays would be constantly poking their sleek, dark heads up alert, looking for the mad squirrel to come charging back, which he did. That squirrel went flying many times. It was the best game of keep away I have seen in all my years.

One morning, the squirrel had it figured out. The squirrel must have dreamed it the night before. He went right to work on the pancake. He began chewing from the pancakes outer edge, straight to the spike.

When he had made the cut to the spike, he went to the other side. He pulled the pancake off the bridge spike, stumbling and hopping away with the whole pancake. Jays followed him, scolding him with the intent to rob him. After that, we cut the pancakes into small parts for all to share the prize. The gray jays earned their nickname Camp Robbers.

This was all recorded on film as it happened, and I still enjoy watching the DVDs today.

One day, we saw the squirrel on the top of a short stick in front of the entrance of the dugout, nibbling on a grouse's feathered skin that Jeff had put outside. Or perhaps he had left it where he had field dressed the grouse.

What is that squirrel doing? Knitting a scarf? We watched and could see he was chewing the fat (no pun intended) off the skin, hand over hand, with the feathers dangling. When he was done with the fat removal, he began to stuff the feathers into his cheeks. He was most likely doing this for nesting material.

During one of my recordings, with the camcorder on to watch the falling of the birch trees for the purpose of making lumber, the tripod was nearly flattened by a falling tree. This near miss happened when the camcorder had been set up to run by itself, at a considerably safe distance. I had set it up on the ridge overlooking the area that I was falling trees for the saw logs. Apparently it wasn't far enough.

Sometimes in a dense forest, trees hang up. As they fall, they can come to a rest on another tree before they fall all the way to the ground. The tree went where I wanted it to but got hung up and was resting at a 45-degree angle.

I did not particularly want to be under this hung up tree in order to saw down the supporting tree. (I make deadfall traps like that.) I could see that it was about to continue on to the ground but needed a nudge is all.

These birch trees were big lumber. Ranging anywhere from twelve to twenty-four inches in diameter, they were very tall. They had branches that were so heavy; if one limb broke loose and hit me, it could kill me. These limbs are called widow makers.

Dad taught me about these widow makers at the age of nine, when I helped him make lumber. I surmised this tree that was hung up was too risky to be under. Or even be near it, when it would finally fall. The safest way was to knock it down by dropping a second tree on it, letting the branches and limbs that held it break off.

There were lots of trees of size nearby to drop on this hung up tree. I sawed a second tree, striking the first hard, mid-center of its large trunk. It worked.

Limbs and busted branches flew, but the tree that was struck found a new direction, and the top of it went right toward the camcorder. My heart sunk. A moment later, the treetop fell just short of the rolling camcorder.

Upon viewing the lengthy, and unedited footage, I am very glad the camcorder was not crunched by the falling tree. The following is what I heard, and saw, on the film: After a few moments, I heard myself shout the warning, "*Timber!*" The second tree fell, striking the first, and like dominoes rolling to the side, came right at the lens of the camcorder, whipping the treetops' branches with the recording sound of *whoosh*.

I went on setting up the camcorder to record the making of the lumber on the different sites. I had used a chant hook to roll up the sawed logs on a portable support bench. This made it easy for me to work off the ground, at waist height, saving my back.

It also allowed me to bring the mill to the heavy logs, rather than having to move the logs to the mill. I am a strong believer in the Mark III chain saw mill, a highly portable chain saw mill.

Moving the lumber is easier than moving one log. If you have the means to stack or pile the logs on site, that, too, is an option. Either way, the mill is very versatile.

It helps that I have made my own improved design, a way of shaping and sharpening a chainsaw chain so that it cuts faster than a commercial store-bought ripping chain.

My private, close to the vest–designed chain has no wobbling or wearing of the bar's side groove on its rail. Plus, it extends the life of the chain and leaves a smooth finish on the lumber's surfaces. I have sawed thousands of feet of boards on Ose Mountain.

Also, there was the two days of rebuilding and cleaning a chainsaw's carburetor. I did this in the dugout that had an earth floor. It was the only working chainsaw we had, so I had to get this one back in working order.

This chainsaw's carburetor needed to be taken apart to be cleaned. In the process, a needle valve fell to the dirt floor. Panic set in, nobody move! The search area was contained, and in two days, I had the carburetor back on and the chainsaw running. That was a long two days.

Remember when I wrote about not eating a grouse the first day of the kill? Well, Jeff had a cooler set up just outside the dugout. It was simply a five-gallon covered plastic pail, which was hung up high on the outside wall to keep the field dressed grouses cold and safe from the meat eaters. We were fortunate to eat fresh grouse on a regular basis.

A pine marten is a meat eater. Jeff got one with my instructions. He mixed up its brains, and his brain tanned his own hide. Each animal's brain gray matter has just enough acid in it to tan the animal's hide.

That is something to think about. Our brain is like a battery; do not let it go dry or run down. Our thought power and reasoning comes from our brain, so keep it energized by using it.

17

Last Night in the Dugout

November 10

Our 1986 mission was completed as planned. Well, all except the trapper's cabin. The change of plans worked for the better. Now I had a warm and well-built hole in the ground, known as the Dugout.

Our last night there was a sad night. Nonetheless, we rejoiced fully from the fact that we completed what we had set out to do, right on schedule.

We had finished the ATV trail and built a habitable dwelling that the federal government surely would approve of. Together, Jeff and I outfitted this dwelling, making it something we could be proud of. Shelf space, rifles on the overhead rack, a peg-made table, a double rope bunk, storage space for our tools that would be left behind for the next year, dry wood floor, wood heating stove, and memories recorded for all time on film.

We had made new friends that liked pancakes too, as well as the four-foot-wide door for an ATV, which would be stored in here the following year. We also built the outdoor closed-in toilet, save for the door. But who needs a door in the wilderness? It's good enough as long as it keeps the rain and snow off while comfortably contemplating life sitting on the throne. My Cousin Owen Ose calls this outhouse "the room with a view."

This last night with the camcorder rolling, I worked the door by opening it and closing it. I was looking out there into the darkness. At that very moment, the radio station 104 KKLV out of Anchorage played the song "Somewhere Out There." How fitting.

Early the next morning, we packed up our bed rolls, some food, and our backpacks. We closed the door and locked it with the burl trick lock. We made our way down to the Frenchman's cabin, the base camp at the lake.

There we would be picked up by a prearranged flight. It was arranged back on the 23rd of August. We would be flown to Fairbanks, where we'd be buying a bucket of KFC for the long drive back to Wood Lake, Minnesota.

At base camp, we put our stuff out on the lake ice, near the new dock we had built early on, to use the following year. Now all we could do was to wait for the plane. Jeff was getting worried by late afternoon when no plane had yet arrived.

Jeff had his mind fixed on that plane to be here. I reassured him it would be here. Praying it would be, all the while, trying not to show my worries too.

"Listen! Hear that? Da plane! Da plane!" It was finally here. We got in it and were on our way to Fairbanks, then on down the Alaskan Canadian Highway to Minnesota.

Next year, 1987, I *would* be back, to continue building on Ose Mountain.

For you see, this is not, *the end.*

18

Now for a Special Added Chapter by Jeff Peterson

I originally met Duane when I was fourteen and working at the local grocery store in Wood Lake, Minnesota. I knew nothing of his past or any of his family. I just saw him a couple times a month. He would come in wearing a green hard hat and goggles. I never knew why he wore the goggles or the eyeglasses with only the one clear lens.

I could see others avoiding him, or looking at him while whispering to someone else. Eventually, I met his son Dan. After a less-than-friendly encounter, we both ended up laughing, and a friendship was born.

It was shortly after that I learned Duane was Dan's dad. Over the years, Dan and I became better friends. I eventually learned of Duane's gunshot wound. Dan and I both enjoyed hikes through the woods at their woodlot.

We would spend many nights camping and fishing together. Soon, I was invited along on local fishing trips with Duane and Dan. I learned a lot from Duane on those fishing trips and not necessarily all fishing knowledge either.

Duane was a father-type figure to me. He would learn about the shenanigans pulled by his son and me, but never judged. Although, he did, however, give me insight to the better style of life.

I had moved out of my parent's house when I was seventeen and started drinking pretty heavily. There was not much to do in a town of four hundred, so partying became my pastime. This was interrupted by numerous fishing trips with Duane, sometimes without Dan.

Sorry, Dan, but I appreciated those trips the most, as I felt I could talk to Duane without feeling embarrassed, or worrying about looking a fool. Duane always answered my questions to the best of his abilities, and if you know me at all, I ask a lot of questions. It is the best way to learn.

Duane taught me how to shoot a bow, and I practiced in his backyard quite frequently. The fishing was replaced with deer hunting in the fall, including making a couple of deer stands. We even put one on a high pole by the pond on his parent's farm.

What a scary seat, as were the stories that would come from sitting on that seat, like the sound an arrow makes when striking a wood pallet, placed as a sort of a dock on the shore of the pond.

During my senior year in high school, I enlisted in the marines. I was scheduled to be shipped out January 1987. I was 6'1" and 145 pounds. I needed to gain weight in order to join the Marines, so I began to eat more and drink less.

Duane and I went fishing for monster catfish during the Franklin (Minnesota) Catfish Derby Days, along with Dan, Larry Brau, and a couple other people. We caught several large catfish, but nothing worthy of first place. I had a cap purchased by Duane, in order to remember the event. If you look, you will notice the purple cap in a picture Duane took of me in the wilderness.

During this time, I learned of Duane's upcoming Alaskan adventure to be. I recall saying how I wish I could do something like that. My favorite book of all time is *My Side of the Mountain* by Jean Craighead George. I have always wanted to live like Grizzly Adams, my favorite show on TV, but never gave a thought to actually being able to go.

Before leaving for Alaska, I had a drunken bicycle accident, breaking my glasses. We (Duane and I) could not find a place to get new ones on short notice before we left. That is why I wore the recreational spec, which I eventually broke as well. You might notice in the pictures that they were taped in the center of the frame, using a piece of wood for stability.

I had to pack nothing for myself, except for a heavy quilt and some snacks. I had bought cigarettes, but not enough, and soon went without. As for attire, Duane outfitted me with all the proper clothes, even down to the underwear and socks.

I will always be thankful to Duane. This was a low point in my life, which turned into the best time in my life. He let me select a backpack, one with an external frame that would come in handy later. Duane already had a mountain internal frame pack. Duane's pack, I used in carrying the full 5-gallon gasoline cans up the mountain. Imagine if you will, me walking 3.5 miles uphill, with 2-5 gallon cans in his backpack, a 5-gallon gasoline can in each hand, and a rifle across my arms. Up the hill I went. That was the longest trip up the hill I ever had.

While working on the making of the trail, I had a very physical job of throwing the whole trees into the nooks. Sometimes, I had to force the first few in to create my own spot.

The worst part in the making of this trail was the deadfalls mixed with 2-inch birch saplings, although sometimes those parts created a place to sit, or even shoot supper from. (Those stupid little grouse birds tasted so yummy.) I even ate the livers, gizzards, and hearts. I noticed the stones in their gizzards, a little, white kind of quartz.

Now don't get me wrong, Duane also had a very physical job, bending over to saw the trees day after day, except for the really rainy days. As well as some trips to the other lake, which Duane had so named Talking Lake.

There was also the cutting of firewood, which we used a lot of. Cooking took some time, and on the cool nights, the fire was needed.

I was pretty much in charge of the fire and became more adept at starting it quickly and efficiently. We did have matches, so it was not like I had to use flint and steel, or any of the other versions of fire starting methods.

Building a fire correctly is a skill to learn, and I had a good teacher. I also learned how to control the fire in the stove, after a couple of times having a cherry red stove pipe, due to too much kindling, or small twigs and branches.

Cut Hand

I got up one morning in the Hobo Hut (lean-to), anxious to get a fire going. I was cold and thought I would have a breakfast ready for when Duane woke up. This was, after all, one of my main duties.

There were no coals in the stove, so I needed some easy to light kindling. Not having much light in the lean-to, I decided to do this in the dark. I did not want to wake Duane early for no reason. I had done this many times before.

I was able to quickly, and fairly quietly, get a fire going before Duane was up. I grabbed the double bit ax because it was sharp. Holding the dry wood in my left hand, I would place the ax on one end of this length of firewood to cleave off small cooking wood. I raised the wood and ax up, then let it go, bouncing the wood on the dirt floor, repeating this.

One particular time, I inadvertently placed the ax right on a knot. (I found this out by looking at it in the light.) Well, things didn't quite go as planned. The ax was narrow and sharp. Duane had sharpened it well.

The ax bounced off the hard knot and landed directly on the knuckle of my left index finger, slicing through the flesh and into the bone. Not wanting to look, I wrapped it with a piece of towel and continued making cooking wood using the same method.

I thought, *It can't be that bad, I can still bend my finger.* The cooking fire was going well. Duane woke up, and in case you are wondering, no! Breakfast was not ready. He lit the lantern and put on his metaphorical doctor's hat.

Using tweezers, his head cocked close to my hand, he pulled out some bone pieces. Then he said, "We have to disinfect it." We had nothing but bleach. Good Lord, my hand, during the disinfecting, felt like it was on fire.

Having disinfected my hand, our attention went to stopping the bleeding. Compression worked, but any hand movement opened it back up. "I can sew it back up!" Duane said.

I was having no part of that. "No way!"

"Well, I could dump some gunpowder from some .22 bullets, and light it."

I convinced him it would stop on its own. "Let's just bandage it for now and look at it later." Bandage it up he did. This couldn't be a simple Band-Aid. This had to be an around the hand, around the thumb, heavy-duty, bandage job. This was my left hand (for those who don't know, I am left handed), and I needed this hand to finish work. We had lots to do and little time left to do it.

Lean-To to Dugout

The outside of the cabin (dugout), minus the door, was built. The interior needed lots of work. It was, after all, a lean-to in the beginning. It was a place to bring the stove in, to have heat and comfort.

First, I had to level out the back area for a place to sleep. We had hollows that we shaped to our own bodies for the most comfortable sleep. These hollows worked while Duane designed a double rope bunk cut from logs and gave me the specs to build them. I peeled the logs for the bed parts and rails.

Cut Kneecap

While I was peeling a log with Duane's curved log drawknife, I found a thumb-sized branch had been sawed off, leaving a little stump. I decided that if I put some oomph into it, I could slice it off smooth. Boy! Did it!

I sliced right through the stump, and into my left kneecap, literally into it. Duane put some gauze on it and then wrapped it up in toilet paper. Then he basically wrapped it up, creating a cast of duct tape. My knee throbbed for days, but we had work to do.

Outhouse Construction

We started our work on the outhouse, before the dugout was completed. I dug and dug but found less than a vegetable can full of rocks. Now I wondered where the birds got their *grit*. For rocks were few and far between.

There was a cluster of five spruce trees, of which four were used as the corner posts. These were root-based posts, meant for solid corners. Being completely square was not an issue.

The fifth tree was left so I could climb down after completing the roof. The ground had frozen layers of annual frost depths, and each needed a day to thaw before I could dig on down. This meant a day to hunt and explore for me. Above all, having real meat, rather than Spam. Spam is a meat I used to love, but out there in the wilderness, I got sick of it really quickly.

Hobo Hut

Every day, Duane was felling trees to make lumber for the outhouse and the dugout. At the end of the day, I would help him carry back the boards he had made during the day. After supper, we would be busy nailing the boards up inside the dugout. At first, with the dugout covered with poly, it looked to me like a Hobo Hut. Whatever you want to call it, it was *home*. It meant safety, shelter, storage, but most of all, it was home.

Thin Ice

Duane and I were setting out across the lake by the Frenchman's cabin, on to Mark's cabin on Talking Lake. This was sometime in mid-October. I asked Duane, "How thick is the ice?"

He said, "I don't know," then pulled his hunting knife and jabbed it into the ice. The water came gushing up. Duane said, "Step back slowly, follow my same tracks, but keep some distance between us. And step lightly, flat-footed." I was scared and followed his directions; we made it, but took a different way, a land course back.

Living Dead Bird

Duane was videotaping me shooting a spruce grouse that was sitting on a branch in a large spruce tree. I shot, but the bird didn't move. I shot it again. This time, I knew I hit it for sure, as you could see the bird's reaction to the impact of the .22 cal bullets.

The bird did not drop. I kept shooting, I am not sure the number of shots, but I believe it was around seven, before the bird finally dropped. When we got it "home," and I went to clean it, the breast (which is the majority of the meat eaten) was so bullet-riddled that it was inedible. I shot them dead, from then on, with headshots.

Duck on the Water

One of the earliest days at base camp, I was looking at the ducks and thought they would be good to eat. The killing was the easiest part. Then the wind died, leaving the dead duck far out from shore. The water was extremely cold, next to freezing. It took me hours to get that duck by snaring it with a fishing line. So that was the last duck I shot, and I found out what dogs are good for. Boy! That duck was good to eat though.

My Golden Forest Cabin

I remember a spot in the Golden Forest, where I wanted to build my own cabin. As Duane had told me I could build my own cabin, and I was welcome up there for as long as I wanted. I wish I had done this and had the means to live out there. Duane and I made a great team.

(DAO note: It would have to have been a squatter's cabin, as the Federal Land Opening was closing, before Jeff would have time to file. He is always welcome here.)

Caged Marten

Duane shot a marten with the .22 rifle, wounding it, but only stunning it. He saw in that marten an opportunity to have a pet, to save the animal and train it. I quickly made a wooden box cage and nursed the marten back to health. We kept him inside the dugout. A few days had passed. Duane decided it was time to release him, as he was now healthy. He was friendly enough to have the run of the dugout, acting like he was one of us, in much the same manner as a pet house cat.

For days to follow, the marten had the run of the dugout, inside and outside. Then one day, the marten, while on Duane's lap, for some reason went off like a bomb. Spraying like a skunk, it went crazy.

Realizing he had done wrong, he ran off and hid in the walls of the dugout. We tore part of the wall apart and dispatched him, then aired the place out. Duane never knew until then that they are like a skunk and are very sensitive. Anything can set them off like a bomb. Duane meant well, but now I had a marten to skin.

Marten

Time was short, so a wall hanger the marten skin would be. I skinned that marten, dried the skin, and, with its brains, tanned the pelt. Duane told me how to tan by using the animal's brains, telling me the brains of each animal is enough to tan its own hide. Working the skin on a sharpened edge of a breaker board opens the pores, to allow the rubbing in of the mushed, beaten up brains. This is to make the pelt soft and subtle so that it can be used as garment material, or a wall hanger.

Bridge over Deep Water

Then there was the first trip to Mark's cabin. We came upon a deep narrow span of water; it was the outlet of Talking Lake. Duane said we could find a place down further to cross but decided we could build a quick walking bridge. "It might take some time now, but it will save us time in the future. The span is not all that wide, and there are some dry fire killed deadfalls we could use nearby." We dragged three stout, long poles, to the edge of the creek, and Duane went on downstream. He crossed over and came back up to the other side. One by one, I pushed the bridge poles over to him. Then one by one, he raised his ends up out of the water, placing them on the bank.

Duane told me to find some long, small poles to push into the mud bottom every so often. Snugging them up to the one side of these three, placed together bridge poles. I tossed two long, small poles over to his side. Together, we pushed the poles deep into the mud bottom. We now had a footbridge and a steady rest. It was scary, but we managed to cross the lake a few times without falling in. It wasn't a forever bridge, but it worked and saved us time. He dubbed it the Bridge over the River Qui.

Living the Dream

My list of memories goes on and on. The beauty I saw was breathtaking and surreal, the new experiences daily. Thank you, thank you, thank you! I so want to do it again. It's just that life gets in the way!

19

A Poem by Jeff Peterson
"Reminisce"

So I was asked to write a chapter
Detailing what I can remember
To sum it up, it was great fun
Though it was a rough September!

The freezing rain, the frozen pants
The Sun came up, another chance
A chance to prepare and do it quick
Please, Duane, show me the trick!

The wildlife we would always hear
Sometimes we would see it too
Sometimes it would be our supper
Always thinking what all we should do!

We used our heads, our muscles too
There was so much, so much to do!
A hobo hut it was, we called it a lean-to
What do we need next; we need a place to poo!
I did all Duane asked of me

At times I had my doubts
But prepared he was and most of all
We never went without

Lean-to always needed something to be done
But work like this isn't bad it's even kind of fun.
You learn to do so many things through error or success
You learn a marten in a cage can really make a mess.

The lakes were freezing over now
The food was running low
Now we were preparing
For it was time to go!

It was a sad day for me
That solid door pushed shut
And over the ridge and down the hill
And to Frenchman's hut.

I only dared to look back once
And yes a tear did fall
I felt that I had left behind
The most awesome place of all

Thanks, Duane, the Mountain Man
The friend he's always been
For all he's done, for all I learned
And all that I have seen.

One time again I hope to see
The land I helped him on
To shake his hand and reminisce
I could go on and on

Thee End

ABOUT THE AUTHOR

Duane is new to the writing world but not new to the world of experience. He was born and raised in Minnesota, in country overlooking the river valley. Duane graduated from Echo High School in 1960. In 1964, he joined the army, at the age of twenty-one. He spent three years in the army, one of those years he spent stationed in South Korea, working as a US army engineer.

Duane is married, has three children, and six grandchildren. He started his own company in the Minnesota farming area selling and delivering concrete. Duane was a scoutmaster, is a survival expert, and is skilled at living and thriving under some of the most extreme conditions known to man.

He's also a public speaker, giving presentations on off grid living, homesteading, survival, Alaskan living, and interesting topics such as the art of dowsing. Duane moved to Alaska on a whim nearly thirty years ago, after surviving a shot in the head. His wife Rena and he became the last persons to have filed a claim under the Federal Homestead Act of 1862. The Homestead Act of 1862 ended for good October 1986.

Duane found his second wife through a mail-order bride system, and married Rena, of Hamilton, Canada. Rena moved to the Alaskan homestead to live in a hole in the ground, called a dugout, for nine years, while she and Duane built their three-story log home.

They live off the land for the most part, by gardening, using solar power, and trapping. Rena does the skinning. Duane has so named their heaven on earth Ose Mountain.

Duane has now taken to writing and has plans for writing several books while living in their log home on Ose Mountain. Rena will have a book out soon as well, on wild game preparation and cooking. One thing Duane wrote while living in the dugout one winter day is a poem titled "River Days Past."

A TV interview of Duane and Rena Ose on Ose Mountain, completed in 2010, can be viewed at: https://www.youtube.com/watch?v=4uurXp8aOps&t=12s